PRAISE FOR *HIS M*

"In *His Mighty Strength*, Randy doesn't just teach us about God's power, he shows us God's power made perfect in his personal wounds and weakness. His vulnerability empowers us all to trust that God can take our surrender and our obedience and move mountains we're powerless to move on our own."

—DAVE RAMSEY, BESTSELLING AUTHOR AND RADIO HOST

"You may feel stuck and powerless, but don't give up hope. Go on a deliberate journey with Randy Frazee as he teaches what Jesus teaches and leads where Jesus leads. You will find power not in your own strength, but in the only One with might."

—KYLE IDLEMAN, SENIOR PASTOR OF SOUTHEAST CHRISTIAN CHURCH; AUTHOR OF *NOT A FAN* AND *DON'T GIVE UP*

"Have you ever felt powerless in your life? In *His Mighty Strength*, Randy Frazee shows how God continues to use us in the midst of our weakness to further display the power of Christ. This is not a watered-down self-help book—this is a powerful gospel-centered guide to walking in the fullness of Christ."

—FRANCESCA BATTISTELLI, GRAMMY AWARD–WINNING SINGER-SONGWRITER

"If I could afford to buy only one car right now, it would be the Polestar. If I could buy only one book right now, it would be this one, a gentle masterpiece on the Polestar Light of Christ that orients us forward as it embraces, empowers, and emboldens us through life's mazes and messes. With courageous vulnerability and unflinching transparency, Frazee has written a great book for this grueling moment. And a great book is not one you review, but respect, revere, and salute."

—LEONARD SWEET, DISTINGUISHED PROFESSOR AT DREW UNIVERSITY, PORTLAND SEMINARY, EVANGELICAL SEMINARY, AND TABOR COLLEGE; BESTSELLING AUTHOR OF *RINGS OF FIRE*; FOUNDER OF PREACHTHESTORY.COM AND SALISH SEA PRESS

"My life has been deeply impacted over the years by the encouragement and teaching of my friend Randy Frazee. His gift of communication and his deep knowledge of Scripture have combined over and over again to bring people like me closer in my relationship with the Lord. Once again, God has given Randy a powerful message for such a time as this. A message that will speak loudly to a weary world that desperately needs to remember where our true source of strength is found."

—MATTHEW WEST, AWARD-WINNING SINGER-SONGWRITER

"If empowerment is on your prayer list, I highly recommend you read this book."

—MARK BATTERSON, LEAD PASTOR OF NATIONAL COMMUNITY CHURCH; *NEW YORK TIMES* BESTSELLING AUTHOR OF *THE CIRCLE MAKER*

"This is the right book for the right time! There isn't a believer out there who doesn't need an extra dose of superpower in their life."

—TIM HARLOW, SENIOR PASTOR OF PARKVIEW CHRISTIAN CHURCH; AUTHOR OF *WHAT MADE JESUS MAD?*

"When discouragement sets in, sadness takes over, frustration mounts, and loneliness prevails, Randy Frazee reminds us that we're destined for more. No matter where you are in life, God wants to take you on a journey that will empower your hope in him."

—CALEB KALTENBACH, DIRECTOR OF THE MESSY GRACE GROUP; AUTHOR OF *MESSY GRACE*

"A rich book for a long-overdue spiritual conversation about powerlessness and mental health [that] you will always find yourself coming back to as you move through the seasons of life."

—CAYLIN LOUIS MOORE, AUTHOR OF *A DREAM TOO BIG*

"*Finally*! Someone says more than just we *have* the power of the resurrection. They tell us *how* to access the power of the resurrection!"

—RUSTY GEORGE, PASTOR OF REAL LIFE CHURCH; AUTHOR OF *AFTER AMEN*

"This is an anti-autobiography, by which I mean this is Randy's story of learning to surrender himself to God by learning that in powerlessness we can align with God's will and be empowered by God's Spirit and live in the very power that raised Jesus from the dead."

—SCOT MCKNIGHT, PROFESSOR OF NEW TESTAMENT AT NORTHERN SEMINARY; AUTHOR OF *THE KING JESUS GOSPEL* AND *THE JESUS CREED*

"I love how vulnerable and transparent Randy gets in the pages of this book. He grabs your attention—not just with well-crafted words and powerful principles (which he certainly does), but by conveying how it feels to go through seasons of betrayal and despair [and] how those seasons of pain provide opportunities to tap into the power Jesus gave his life for us to have."

—AARON BROCKETT, PASTOR OF TRADERS POINT CHRISTIAN CHURCH

"This book is one for all of us who need to know how to 'walk daily in the same power that raised Jesus from the dead,' written by a man who did that in one of the most difficult seasons of his life."

—CHUCK BOOHER, LEAD PASTOR OF CROSSROADS CHURCH; AUTHOR OF *ISAIAH: THE BOOK OF THE KING*

"*His Mighty Strength* is a powerful book that offers hope and encouragement to anyone facing struggles or discouragement in their daily life. If you're tired of settling for a powerless life when God offers so much more, you will benefit from reading this book. It is a must-read!"

—PHIL HOPPER, LEAD PASTOR OF ABUNDANT LIFE; AUTHOR OF *THE WEAPONS OF OUR WARFARE*

"If you have ever felt powerless or lost, then you will want to read this book. Once again [Randy] has written a book that is applicable to all of our lives."

—STEVE POE, SENIOR PASTOR OF NORTHVIEW CHURCH; AUTHOR OF *CREATURES OF HABIT*

"This book is powerful because Randy writes personally and authentically about one of his darkest seasons. My guess is, as you turn the pages, God will help you turn a corner to finally live in his power and freedom."

—ASHLEY WOOLDRIDGE, SENIOR PASTOR OF CHRIST'S CHURCH OF THE VALLEY

"In *His Mighty Strength*, Randy's transparency and vulnerability will plow the road for the Word of God to get through to the tender places of your heart. Read the introduction and it will be 'game over.' You'll be in until the end."

—JERRY HARRIS, SENIOR PASTOR OF THE CROSSING;
PUBLISHER OF *CHRISTIAN STANDARD* MAGAZINE

"The biblical principles taught in this book have transformed [Randy's] life and mine, and it will transform yours as well."

—ANDREW LOKE, ASSOCIATE PROFESSOR AT HONG KONG BAPTIST
UNIVERSITY; AUTHOR OF *A KRYPTIC MODEL OF THE INCARNATION*

"We have all had dark nights of the soul, but what do you do when you have a dark *season* of the soul and you don't see the way forward? Randy is not only transparent about that season, but he gives the tools to move forward through the person and power of Jesus."

—SHANE PHILIP, SENIOR PASTOR OF THE CROSSING

"In this book, through his extreme honesty and vulnerability, my friend Randy shares his own struggles to see God when it's dark outside."

—CAL JERNIGAN, LEAD PASTOR OF CENTRAL CHRISTIAN CHURCH

"I needed this book. Every day, my heart looked forward to opening it and continuing this journey that Randy was on. A journey that I was on as well, though I didn't even realize it."

—TIM LISTON, LEAD PASTOR OF NEW HOPE CHURCH

"*His Mighty Strength* is a gift for anyone who has ever struggled with how to channel the miraculous resurrection power we read about in Scripture into our current challenges. Randy's personal journey is not only relatable but will fill you with new hope and strength."

—GENE APPEL, SENIOR PASTOR OF EASTSIDE CHRISTIAN CHURCH

HIS
Mighty
STRENGTH

ALSO BY RANDY FRAZEE

What Happens After You Die

The Heart of the Story

Think, Act, Be Like Jesus

Believe (general editor)

The Christian Life Profile Assessment

The Connecting Church 2.0

Believe 365 Day Devotional
(coauthored with Rozanne Frazee)

Real Simplicity (coauthored with
Rozanne Frazee)

Renovation of the Heart,
Student Edition (coauthored
with Dallas Willard)

HIS
Mighty
STRENGTH

WALK DAILY *in the* SAME POWER THAT
RAISED JESUS FROM THE DEAD

RANDY FRAZEE

NELSON
BOOKS

An Imprint of Thomas Nelson

Published in Nashville, Tennessee, by Nelson Books, an imprint of Thomas Nelson. Nelson Books and Thomas Nelson are registered trademarks of HarperCollins Christian Publishing, Inc.

Published in association with Don Gates of the literary agency The Gates Group - www.thegates-group.com.

Thomas Nelson titles may be purchased in bulk for educational, business, fundraising, or sales promotional use. For information, please e-mail SpecialMarkets@ThomasNelson.com.

Any internet addresses, phone numbers, or company or product information printed in this book are offered as a resource and are not intended in any way to be or to imply an endorsement by Thomas Nelson, nor does Thomas Nelson vouch for the existence, content, or services of these sites, phone numbers, companies, or products beyond the life of this book.

ISBN 978-0-7180-8612-1 (TP)
ISBN 978-0-7180-8613-8 (eBook)
ISBN 978-0-310-63523-9 (CU)

Library of Congress Cataloging-in-Publication Data

Names: Frazee, Randy, author.
Title: His mighty strength : walk daily in the same power that raised Jesus from the dead / Randy Frazee.
Description: Nashville : Thomas Nelson, 2021. | Includes bibliographical references. | Summary: "Popular pastor Randy Frazee shows Christians how to walk day by day in the resurrection power that Jesus experienced"-- Provided by publisher.
Identifiers: LCCN 2020034200 (print) | LCCN 2020034201 (ebook) | ISBN 9780718086121 (paperback) | ISBN 9780718086138 (epub)
Subjects: LCSH: Power (Christian theology) | Jesus Christ--Resurrection.
Classification: LCC BT738.25 .F73 2021 (print) | LCC BT738.25 (ebook) | DDC 232/.5--dc23
LC record available at https://lccn.loc.gov/2020034200
LC ebook record available at https://lccn.loc.gov/2020034201

Printed in the United States of America

21 22 23 24 25 LSC 10 9 8 7 6 5 4 3 2 1

To Jim Hilliard
Golf will resume at the resurrection. I love you more.

CONTENTS

STUCK IN THE VALLEY

The first time it happened, the clock on my nightstand read 3:00 a.m. I had woken up in a panic, breathless, beating my pillow with my fist. I covered my face with my hands. *What in the world is going on?* My heartbeat was so strong and so fast I could feel it pulsating in my neck.

I rolled over onto my back, stared at the murky ceiling, and took several deep breaths. *Calm down. It was just a bad dream. Shake it off. Go back to sleep.* But it hadn't been a dream at all. It was a betrayal, one that had been all too real.

Now wide-awake, I watched all the scenes play out across the ceiling like the disaster movie my life had become in the last three months. I rehearsed every decision I'd made or failed to make that had left me blind to the unfolding scheme. I obsessed over every detail of every conversation, every plot twist, every rabbit trail—ad nauseam. Instead of lashing out at those who had betrayed me, I saw every scene as a launchpad for lashing out at myself.

You are so stupid. How could you not see this coming?

What an idiot.

Why are you always so trusting?

It's over for you now. There's no bouncing back from this one.

What a disgusting mess you are. You're completely powerless to pull yourself together.

Then I'd move on to the next scene and lash myself all over again, pounding my fists into my pillow out of anger and self-loathing. After the final scene, which had no happy ending, I went back and started the movie, and the self-flagellations, all over again. When my fist pounding eventually woke my wife, Rozanne, I convinced her I'd just had a bad dream.

The next night, it happened again. The same fist pounding, panic, and breathless awakening. I tried to talk myself down, tried to reason with my frightened psyche for a good five minutes, tried to calmly lay out all the reasons this personal-disaster movie marathon wasn't helping the situation one bit. But my psyche wasn't buying it and was determined that I would watch the movie, pound on my pillow, and mentally beat the crud out of myself until the pain somehow stopped. I felt powerless to do anything but go along.

I'm not a violent man. Hitting in any form is not my vice. But I was in a darker place than I had ever been before, a place of trauma, and I had no road map to help me escape. Once again, my fist pounding woke up Rozanne. "Cut it out," she said sleepily as she rolled over.

The next night, like clockwork, it happened again. This time, I actually wanted to wake up Rozanne on purpose because I was frightened and didn't want to be alone in the madness.

What is happening to me?

Where is this going?

I'm not the only person who has experienced this kind of trauma, so why can't I let it go?

Snap out of it already.

But I couldn't snap out of it, and I felt powerless in the face of my own pain. I was not on a good path, and I knew it. I wanted to turn things around, but I couldn't. It felt as if I was being drawn deeper and deeper into a dark vortex and I couldn't do anything to stop it. I was relieved when the pillow-beating wake-up calls stopped after a few more nights, but they weren't the first sign I was in trouble.

"You don't sing anymore," Rozanne said one day about two weeks after the betrayal. Anybody who has been around me for even a week knows that if I'm not talking, I'm singing. Almost always worship songs. For years, listening to and singing worship songs had been one of my favorite resources for overcoming obstacles. A good worship song could fire me up and give me the power I needed to scale a mountain, walk through a fiery furnace, slay a Goliath, or face off with the Devil himself. Rozanne suggested I try to sing again. So I tried. But nothing happened. I couldn't do it. My spiritual laryngitis would continue for months to come.

I also lost my ability to connect with friends and family. For decades we'd hosted weekly dinners in our home for neighbors and other guests. I'd actually written books about it, and the *New York Times* once did a front-page article on our table experience. Rozanne prepared the food, and I facilitated the conversation. I loved these gatherings and always looked forward to them, but now, as everyone sat around our table laughing and talking, I felt wordless and empty. My funk was literally changing the culture we'd worked so hard to build in our neighborhood and home. I was starting to pull my family and friends down with me into my pit, which only intensified my pain and feelings of powerlessness.

Speaking of food, I lost my appetite for it. I actually lost my willpower to eat. When some people go through hard seasons, they binge eat. Turns out, I stop eating. Rozanne tried to entice me back to food by making some of my favorite dishes, but I wasn't biting.

Another item on my "lost" list was my drive and desire to succeed. Since the age of fourteen I had valued productivity and achievement. I always set annual goals against a five-year vision and then tackled strategic assignments each day to catalyze success. But suddenly I was finding it hard to even get off the sofa.

About two months into this new normal, Rozanne approached me, looking concerned. "Randy," she said, "if you keep this up, it's going to ruin us financially." We were well taken care of by my work, but if I didn't start producing, things would eventually come crashing down. I understood and agreed with her, but I felt powerless to do anything about it. I was trapped in a deep valley of despair and saw no way out.

By the time the late-night pillow-beating episodes hit the three-month mark, I knew I had to do something. It was time to see a doctor—actually, more than one. I desperately reached out to a host of doctors, all Christians: a primary care physician, a licensed counselor, a psychologist, and a psychiatrist.

The first assignment they gave me was to exercise. This actually wasn't too hard to do. I'd been an avid runner for nearly three decades, and I knew full well that exercise released God-given endorphins that could create a sense of peace in the body. So I started a new routine. Instead of running three times a week, I ran three miles twice a day. As I ran, I begged God to heal me. Before I knew it, I'd lost twenty pounds. It's amazing what exercise combined with loss of appetite can do. The weight loss and added muscle tone were certainly health benefits, but they didn't do anything to jolt me out of my depression.

My counselor and a few friends encouraged me to meet with the four people who had betrayed me. So I started setting up appointments. I met with the first one by myself. Big mistake. I experienced it as a meeting of mind games, and it sent me even deeper into the abyss. For my meeting with the second betrayer, who was really more of an accomplice, I brought along a trusted friend. At this meeting, the betrayer unintentionally revealed the truth about what had happened, much as Jack Nicholson's character, Colonel Jessup, did in *A Few Good Men*. This was when I was finally able to stop blaming myself. This whole situation wasn't my fault. There was no decision I could have made that would have prevented the betrayal. Beating my pillow at night and berating myself was for naught. The revelation didn't stop the nightly movie marathons, but it did shift the theme from self-blaming to the betrayal itself. But even this knowledge didn't fix me. Actually, I think I might have recovered faster if everything *had* been my fault. In counseling I discovered that betraying someone who deeply trusted you is one of the most painful wounds one human being can inflict on another. At this point, I decided not to meet with the two remaining betrayers.

"Randy, you are definitely clinically depressed," my psychiatrist said. I was now six months into the fallout from this disaster, and my doctor's words meant I was nowhere near being done with this nightmare I was living in. She prescribed stronger medicines, meds I knew were highly addictive. Once I started taking them, I couldn't just decide to one day stop taking them. I'd have to wean myself off slowly. This frightened me, but the fact that my doctor considered my condition severe enough to warrant such powerful medication frightened me even more.

When it was time to take the first pill, I hesitated. I didn't want to take it, but I also felt I had no alternative. Rozanne stood by my side at the kitchen counter as I held the small white pill in my hand. My body shook, and I began to cry. I wrapped my arms around Rozanne as my knees buckled. "Dear God," I prayed, "help me."

Finally, I swallowed the first pill. After ten days of pills and no sign of change, the doctor concluded this was not the medicine for me after all.

How many more pills do I have to take before I find something that works?

Is this my new normal?

Is this how my story ends?

Here's the kicker. All of this was happening while I was under contract to write a book on experiencing God's resurrection power in our lives. Here I was, writing a book on how to tap into the same power that raised Jesus from the dead, and I could barely raise myself off the couch. Either the premise of the book was a farce or, at the very least, I didn't have a clue about how to experience it. Either way, I now felt disqualified to write the book. I tried numerous times to jump-start my pen, but to no avail. The irony was not, and is not, lost on me.

HOW EMPOWERED ARE YOU?

Powerless. Have you ever felt this way? Are you feeling this way right now? Is it why you picked up this book in the first place? If so, you probably didn't see my story coming, did you? To be honest, I certainly didn't see it coming either. In fact, I'm a bit embarrassed. And yet I also know that I'm far from alone. Even if it doesn't reach the level of clinical depression, all of us experience powerlessness at some point in our lives. And for some of us it may even be a chronic condition. We've gotten so used to feeling powerless in the face of our circumstances, our suffering, or our self-defeating behaviors, that we no longer believe there's an alternative.

So, let me ask you, how empowered is your life right now? If you were to plot yourself on a scale of 1 to 10, what number would you choose on the empowerment scale?

EMPOWERMENT SCALE

1	2	3	4	5	6	7	8	9	10

I Am Powerless	I Am Somewhere Between	I Am Empowered

Before my depression, I would have said I was an 8. In the middle of the mess, I would have said a 2. The distance between those two numbers is called a freefall, by the way.

If you located yourself in the range of 1 to 3, I believe my descent toward powerlessness has made this a better book, and one I hope you can relate to. I am more than just sympathetic to your struggles—I am a member of your support group. Come on this journey with me. I promise not to fill it with clichés or happy talk. No "Pick yourself up by your bootstraps," no "Just choose joy," no "When God closes a door, he opens a window." This is a meaty book, biblically, and I am a teacher of Scripture at my very core. But because of my personal experience in powerlessness, I am also stepping out from behind the pulpit and into that quiet corner of the coffee shop across the table from you, where I hope what I write might feel a bit more like a conversation. No judgment here. Just a heads-up that I believe things can change for you, even if you can't believe that for yourself just yet.

If you chose a number in the range of 4 to 6, welcome to the club. Most people I know place themselves somewhere in the middle, between monotony and mundaneness. You may not have any major trauma in your life at the moment, but each day is essentially a repeat of the day before. Perhaps my story weirded you out a bit. You don't feel quite that powerless, but you certainly don't feel you have any supernatural juices flowing through your veins either. You may be bored. You may have resigned yourself to the idea that this is all there is. Go to work, pay the bills, pass the mashed potatoes, expect to be disappointed, live for the weekend, and push through. You may even have settled comfortably into this way of life.

If you're living in the middle, my promise to you is that there is more to life with God than you're currently experiencing. This is not a "rah-rah" speech. Quite the contrary. There is real hope and real help to move you from the boring middle into a life of power. You don't have to settle.

Now, if you plotted yourself in the range of 7 to 10, that's awesome! Does it mean you should just close up this book and pass it on to a friend less empowered than you? Not so fast. Remember, I would have assessed myself as a 7 or 8 before I hit the free fall that dropped me to a 1 or 2. The same thing can happen to you. I want you to be better equipped than I was and possibly avoid similar trauma altogether.

Also consider that your self-assessment, like mine, is based on what you might have assumed are the limits of what's possible. I thought I saw the empowerment ceiling and felt I was only a few points away from having it all. In this book, I hope to blow through that false ceiling and introduce you to a whole new stratosphere of possibilities. Why would you take a pass on that? It's what God intended for you.

NEW POWER, NEW POSSIBILITIES

The promise of this book is that new power and new possibilities are available to you no matter where you find yourself on the empowerment scale. What might be included on the list of possibilities? Here is just a small sampling:

- the power to forgive someone who has deeply hurt or betrayed you

- the power to get through a difficult situation with dignity
- the power to come alongside a friend or even a stranger who's struggling and make things better for them
- the power to stamp out fear and rise above negative circumstances
- the power to love more deeply
- the power to persevere with grace in a difficult relationship
- the power to expand your influence and experience more victories
- the power to discover and live out God's purpose for your life
- the power to be a conduit for God's miracles
- the power to move mountains of impossibility
- and best of all, in the end, the power to rise from the dead, just as Jesus did

The power that makes all of this possible is centered in the life of Jesus. He is going to open the way for us to tap into his mighty strength by showing us how to walk daily in the same power that raised him from the dead.

You'll notice that the book is divided into three parts, each of which corresponds to key themes in the life of Christ—emptied, aligned, empowered. In part 1, we'll explore the life of Jesus from the time he left his heavenly seat next to the Father until he returned thirty-three years later. The Scriptures tell us that Jesus *emptied* himself when he came to earth. In reading about what this meant for him, I believe you will discover things about Jesus you may never have known before. I hope it will make your love for him and awe of him only grow deeper. Then we'll consider our own story and the ways in which we might need to empty ourselves in order to experience the power promised to us. Be prepared for a little paradigm shift.

In part 2, we'll focus on how Jesus *aligned* himself with God. The pattern of Jesus' life is one in which he intentionally surrendered his will to the will of the Father. Once again, he is going to invite us to do the same. We will ask two very important questions: *How do we know the will of God?* and *How do we hear God's voice?* Be aware before you start this part of the book that though *surrender* is a countercultural idea, it is absolutely critical to access the mighty power that fueled everything Jesus said and did.

In part 3, we'll build on the principles from parts 1 and 2 and explore how we can experience the same power that raised Jesus from the dead. We will look at how this worked for Jesus and then how this works in our lives. This section is all about being *empowered*. It is all about rising above our circumstances and living in victory over life and even death.

Now, here is where the challenge comes in for both of us. Something is required of us. In order to access the power that raised Jesus from the dead, we need to follow the pattern of life that Jesus lived.

The power you need is available to you. Yet you still have to reach out for it. You have to want it. You have to allow hope to have a tiny plot of earth in your heart. You have to believe that things can and will be different for you. If you are not there yet, maybe you will be as you turn the page and begin this journey with me.

So, where am I on that scale today? We'll get there in time. But spoiler alert: I did finish a book on walking daily in the same power that raised Jesus from the dead. Just saying.

PART I

Emptied

CHAPTER 1

WHAT JESUS LEFT BEHIND

Not too long ago, my wife, Rozanne, and I made dinner plans with good friends we hadn't seen in a long time. Because this was such a special occasion, we made reservations at a restaurant that was fancy—and expensive—at least by our standards. We were so excited to reconnect with our good friends, to retell old stories, to catch up on the latest gossip, to laugh and cry, all over a great meal.

The evening turned out to be all that and more. With our hearts and stomachs full, we asked for the check. When it arrived, I reached into my coat pocket to retrieve my wallet, only to discover I had accidentally left it at home. Talk about embarrassed! I had to stick the entire bill on our good friends—well, they used to be good friends. When I got home, I wrote a check and mailed it, not only for our portion, but for the entire cost of the dinner.

This little episode, as humiliating as it was at the time, provides a pretty decent analogy for something Jesus did when he made his reservation to come into our world. We might say there was a big "wallet" of divine resources Jesus left at home when he came to earth. The story of what he left behind is perhaps best told in three stanzas of a beautiful and ancient hymn the apostle Paul included in his letter to the believers at Philippi. Each line of each stanza is packed with rich truth about the identity of Jesus Christ.

A HYMN OF IDENTITY—
HUMAN AND DIVINE

To introduce the hymn, Paul began with this admonition: "In your relationships with one another, have the same mindset as Christ Jesus" (Philippians 2:5). It's the "mindset" part we want to focus on here, which is what Paul was describing when he drew upon the hymn. He was about to tell us some important things about the identity and nature of Jesus that not only give us insight into who Jesus is, but also reveal the astounding nature of what he gave up in order to be with us. That matters because what he gave up also reveals something significant about his mindset and the profound vulnerability it required. Ultimately, Jesus' mindset is to be the pattern we are to follow in our own lives—even when we go through seasons of feeling powerless. Keep that in mind as we do a deep dive into this beautiful hymn.

A Divine Dilemma

> Who, being in very nature God,
>> did not consider equality with God something
>> to be used to his own advantage.
> (Philippians 2:6)

Jesus existed before his birth. No one else can make this claim. What is the basis for this declaration? That Jesus is, *in his very nature*, God.

The apostle John declared Jesus' divine preexistence right at the beginning of his gospel:

> In the beginning was the Word, and the Word was with God, and the Word was God. He was with God in the beginning. Through him all things were made; without him nothing was made that has been made. (John 1:1–3)

One of the names given to Jesus before he was called Jesus by Joseph and Mary was the Word. The Word spoke creation into existence in Genesis 1. The entire nativity scene into which Jesus was born was created by him—the stable, the animals, Mary and Joseph, the shepherds, the swaddling clothes in which he was wrapped, the gold, frankincense, and myrrh he received as gifts from the Magi. Everything.

Just to make sure we didn't miss John's first attempt to clue us in on the nature of Jesus, the apostle later reaffirmed it:

> No one has ever gone into heaven except the one who came from heaven—the Son of Man. (3:13)

Jesus' life didn't begin in Mary's womb. He did not come from the seed of a man. Jesus came to us from heaven, already fully in existence as God. John went on to record Jesus' own declaration of his origins, first in a conversation with his disciples and then in an intimate prayer to God, the Father.

> I came from the Father and entered the world; now I am leaving the world and going back to the Father. (16:28)

> And now, Father, glorify me in your presence with the glory I had with you before the world began. (17:5)

Jesus did not begin his earthly life as we did. He came from heaven. He is none other than the second person of the Godhead—the Son. While on earth, Jesus declared his identity more than once, and understanding that identity is extremely important to the rest of the hymn.

After the first line of the Philippians hymn declares that Jesus is in his very nature God, it states that Jesus "did not consider equality with God something to be used to his own advantage" (2:6). Paul was making it clear that Jesus relinquished access to his divine power in order to walk among us as a human being.

What does this mean and why is it such a big deal to Jesus? To answer that, it's important to take a step back and note that, elsewhere, Paul twice spoke of Jesus in connection with Adam (Romans 5:12–19; 1 Corinthians 15:21–49). The first Adam, described in the Genesis creation story, was created by God without sin. As the first of his kind, he stood before God as a representative for all of humanity. However, Adam didn't remain without sin. When he was tempted in the garden by Satan, he fell, and the consequence of this act was banishment from God's presence and, ultimately, death—and it was a consequence suffered by not just Adam but the entire human race he represented (Romans 5:12).

In contrast, Paul described Jesus as the second or last Adam. He is the only other human being to begin his life on earth without sin. Unlike the first Adam, when Jesus was tempted by Satan in the wilderness, he did not fall (Matthew 4:1–11). When we place our faith in Christ, we officially declare that Jesus, the second Adam, is our new representative before God. The physical act of baptism through immersion provides a vivid picture of this. As we are lowered into the water, it symbolizes that we are dying to our association with the first Adam (Romans 6:4). As we are raised out of the water, it symbolizes our new life in association with Jesus, the second and last Adam. In the words of Jesus, we are "born again" (John 3:3).

Summarizing the teachings of an ancient church father named Irenaeus, scholar Roger Olson wrote, "In order to save us Christ had to reverse the sin of Adam in the 'very same formation' as Adam."[1] This simply means that, in order to overturn the consequences of Adam's fall on humanity, Jesus had to become human himself. It is interesting to note that, in contrast to Jesus, who "did not consider equality with God something to be used to his own advantage," the sin of the first Adam is tied directly to his grasping after equality with God. The serpent's temptation was "You will be like God" (Genesis 3:5). As the second Adam, Jesus qualified himself as our representative by reversing the first Adam's disqualification. He did that in part by letting go of his divine privilege so he might properly represent us.

Biblical writers acknowledged Jesus as our representative when they referred to him as our high priest. In the Old Testament, the high priest was the people's representative before God. The writer of Hebrews said this of Jesus:

> For we do not have a high priest who is unable to empathize with our weaknesses, but we have one who has been tempted in every way, just as we are—yet he did not sin. (Hebrews 4:15)

In becoming human, Jesus chose to subject himself to the same limitations we have as human beings. He allowed himself to be tempted as we are tempted, but he did not give in to these temptations. For his role as the second Adam to be effective in undoing the consequences of the fall, he could not have at his disposal on earth all the attributes he possessed in heaven. To possess unlimited access in and through time and space (omnipresence), the full knowledge of God (omniscience), and the full power of God (omnipotence) are tremendous advantages, wouldn't you say? So to represent us—to fully identify with our human weakness and limitations—Jesus made a most remarkable choice. He emptied himself. That is what the second stanza is all about.

A *Son's Decision*

> He made himself nothing
> > by taking the very nature of a servant,
> > being made in human likeness.
> And being found in appearance as a man,
> > he humbled himself
> > by becoming obedient to death—
> > > even death on a cross!
> > (Philippians 2:7–8)

The phrase "he made himself nothing" centers around the Greek word *kenosis*. In other translations it reads, "he emptied himself."[2] Of what precisely did Jesus *empty* himself? The hymn doesn't say explicitly, but as we study the pattern of Jesus' life, it's not hard to find some obvious clues. *The Message* puts it this way:

When the time came, he *set aside the privileges of deity* and took on the status of a slave, became human! (v. 7, emphasis added)

When Jesus left heaven to become a human being, he freely chose to empty himself of "the privileges of deity," or his divine attributes. These attributes are sometimes referred to as the three "omnis."

- Omnipresence (unlimited presence)
- Omniscience (unlimited knowledge)
- Omnipotence (unlimited power)

Jesus willingly left these divine attributes behind. Had he not done so—had he chosen instead to retain his divine privileges—he would have been able to take advantage of his position as God. As such, he could not have reversed the failure of the first Adam. He expressly told us he didn't want to do that for our sakes.

Jesus emptied himself to become fully human, but it's important to understand that Jesus didn't become any less God as a result. In no way and by no means. Instead, two natures—one human and one divine—coexisted in one person. Yet how could that be when the two natures were quite incompatible? God is unlimited by time and space, but humans are limited by both. God knows all things, but humans do not. God has power over all things, but humans do not. How do we reconcile the incompatibilities between these two natures? How could they possibly coexist in one being?

To get at this, let's go back to my humiliating moment in the restaurant. When the bill came, I couldn't pay because I'd left my wallet—my ability to pay—at home. I didn't lose my ability to pay or forfeit it; I just left it at home. The identity on my driver's license and passport was still intact. I was still fully the person people called Randy Frazee—nothing had changed. Once I returned home, I regained possession of my assets. But while I was away, I involuntarily lacked access to my ability to pay.

Something like this is what I believe Jesus did voluntarily—he temporarily surrendered access to his divine assets. In describing what happened when Jesus became fully human, the writer of Hebrews quoted from Psalm 8, which informs us that humans, while highly valued before God, have a status just a little lower than the angels. When Jesus took on flesh, he shifted positions, from being above the angels to being below them. But the writer of Hebrews clarified that it wasn't a forever shift:

> But we do see Jesus, who was made lower than the angels *for a little while*, now crowned with glory and honor because he suffered death, so that by the grace of God he might taste death for everyone. (Hebrews 2:9, emphasis added)

Jesus took on this lower position with us, but it wasn't a permanent thing. It lasted for thirty-three years, and then he was once again exalted above the angels, as we will see in the third stanza of this beautiful hymn.

How exactly did Jesus empty himself of his divine

attributes, and what did that look like while he was on earth? Let's consider each of the omnis, starting with omnipresence.

Omnipresence is the state of being in all places at all times. God's presence—all of him, not just parts of him—is literally everywhere, always. The psalmist attested to this, declaring, "Where can I go from your Spirit? Where can I flee from your presence?" (Psalm 139:7). The prophet Jeremiah quoted God himself as saying, "Who can hide in secret places so that I cannot see them? . . . Do not I fill heaven and earth?" (Jeremiah 23:24).

Before the resurrection, the Bible records no incident in the life of Jesus in which he had any material advantage over other human beings. For Jesus to get from Galilee to Jerusalem, he had to walk, like everyone else—he was not omnipresent. He voluntarily and temporarily emptied himself of omnipresence so he could identify with us in our limitations and yet still show us the way to a truly empowered life.

When it comes to *omniscience*, we get the first clue from the early years of Jesus' life. Although we don't have much information about the years between Jesus' birth and the beginning of his ministry at age thirty, we do have this one-sentence summary in the gospel of Luke:

> Jesus grew in wisdom and in stature and in favor with God and all the people. (Luke 2:52 NLT)

Humans grow in wisdom (at least that is the goal). God, on the other hand, can't grow in wisdom because God is already all-knowing. It must be so. If Jesus is *growing* in wisdom, he is not all-knowing. Jesus left behind his full knowledge—his omniscience—when he became a man so that he had to grow in knowledge and wisdom just as every human being does. He chose to subject himself to the same limits of knowledge we experience as we grow from babies into adults. And this raises some profound questions: What if Jesus wasn't born knowing he was the Messiah? What if he was growing in wisdom, seeking and discovering God's full plan for him progressively each day just as we have to do? These are disruptive questions with potentially radical implications, I know, but what if they're true?

Later in Jesus' ministry he gave us another clue that his knowledge, while on earth, was limited. He began to lay out some of the signs for the end of time as we know it on earth. When the disciples pressed for more details about exactly when the end would come, Jesus replied:

> But about that day or hour no one knows, not even the angels in heaven, nor the Son, but only the Father. (Mark 13:32)

If Jesus had been omniscient while on earth, he would have known the same things as the Father, but in this case, at least, he didn't. This is knowledge he willingly left behind when he came to earth—a sort of self-induced divine amnesia, if you will.

So we have some clues about Jesus surrendering his rights to divine omnipresence and omniscience, but what about his full power as God, his *omnipotence*? Early in Jesus' ministry, he healed a man who was both blind and mute (Matthew 12:22–29). When the people in the crowd suggested that Jesus just might be the Messiah, the jealous religious leaders claimed that Jesus used the power of Satan to perform miracles. Jesus challenged their accusation with this reply:

> If Satan drives out Satan, he is divided against himself. How then can his kingdom stand? . . . But if it is by the Spirit of God that I drive out demons, then the kingdom of God has come upon you. (vv. 26, 28)

If Jesus is God, then he has the same power as the Father and the Holy Spirit to perform miracles like this. And yet, he seemed to acknowledge that he performed miracles not by his own power but by the power of the Holy Spirit. Why did he need the Spirit to help him out? Because he couldn't and didn't perform any miracles on his own. He decided for our sake to leave his omnipotence behind.

Perhaps the most compelling evidence about the limits of Jesus' power is what the Bible reveals about his resurrection from the dead. Here is a clue written by the apostle Peter:

For Christ also suffered once for sins, the righteous for the unrighteous, to bring you to God. He was put to death in the body but made alive in the Spirit. (1 Peter 3:18)

This verse echoes the same truth the apostle Paul stated about the power that raised Jesus from the dead:

That power is the same as the mighty strength he [God] exerted when he raised Christ from the dead and seated him at his right hand in the heavenly realms. (Ephesians 1:19–20)

Jesus rose from the dead on the third day, but he didn't do so in his own power. Once again, Jesus put himself in a vulnerable position. He went to the cross knowing he could not raise himself from the dead. He was in every way as limited as we are.

These are just a few of the clues from the life of Christ that help us answer the question, Of what did Jesus empty himself? The answer is, he emptied himself of omnipresence, omniscience, omnipotence—everything that made him equal to God. Jesus chose to exchange his divine assets for human limitations. That is the "kenosis transaction."

Just to be clear, when Jesus emptied himself, it does not mean that he *lost* his divine attributes; he merely left them at home—something like I did with my wallet. Once he returned to his heavenly home thirty-three years later, he placed these attributes back into his pocket, if you will. This is precisely how the third stanza of this beautiful hymn ends.

A Father's Declaration

> Therefore God exalted him to the highest place
> and gave him the name that is above
> every name,
> that at the name of Jesus every knee should bow,
> in heaven and on earth and under the earth,
> and every tongue acknowledge that Jesus Christ
> is Lord,
> to the glory of God the Father.
> (Philippians 2:9–11)

Jesus is right now sitting at the right hand of the Father in heaven with full access to his omnipresence, omniscience, and omnipotence. He is no longer bound by time and space as we are. Once again, his presence fills the heavens and the earth. The first sign of this happened right after the resurrection. Jesus suddenly appeared alongside two of his followers who were walking along a road from Jerusalem to Emmaus. Mark's gospel tells us Jesus "appeared in a different form" and the two travelers did not recognize him (Mark 16:12). In Luke's gospel, we are told that once Jesus' identity was revealed to the two,

Jesus "disappeared from their sight" (Luke 24:31). They immediately rushed back to Jerusalem to tell the disciples what had happened. While they were still telling the story, Jesus miraculously appeared among them (v. 36). The time and space limits Jesus endured for thirty-three years had been lifted. He reclaimed his omnipresence.

Jesus once again knows the exact day and time of his return to earth at the end of time. He also knows the thoughts and intents of our hearts (Hebrews 4:12). Jesus knows and is committed to fulfilling every promise he has made. He remembers them all, including the one to come back for us and take us to the place he has prepared for us in the eternal kingdom (John 14:1–4). He has reclaimed his omniscience.

All power is once again in the full grasp of Jesus. The Bible tells us he will use this mighty power to establish his eternal kingdom (Revelation 19:11–16). At that time, Jesus will create a new heaven and a new earth in all of its splendor; the curse of the first Adam has been forever removed (21:1–2). He has reclaimed his omnipotence.

Philippians 2:6–11, written in about AD 60, is a beautiful and magnificent hymn that expresses the depth of Christ's commitment to restoring our relationship with God and showing us how to live an empowered life.

When Jesus emptied himself, he put himself in a vulnerable position—the same position we are in as human beings. And yet, his vulnerability didn't leave him powerless. Instead, it made him wholly reliant on the power of the Holy Spirit. If we want to tap into that same power, the best place to start might be to consider our own vulnerability. This is an essential component of the mindset the apostle Paul invited his readers to have as part of his introduction to the hymn. Jesus intentionally put himself in a powerless position and yet experienced unprecedented power in and through his life, from miracles to a resurrection from the dead. Jesus tells us that we can experience the same thing in our position of powerlessness, and he is going to show us how. But first, we have to have the right mindset—the mindset of Jesus, who emptied himself and chose vulnerability.

OUR POWERLESSNESS

If you or someone you know has ever struggled with an addiction, you're probably familiar with the recovery program developed by Alcoholics Anonymous called the Twelve Steps. The first step is, "We admitted we were powerless over alcohol—that our lives had become unmanageable."[3] That's a good starting place for us as well—to admit our powerlessness to do anything about our own powerlessness.

This certainly rings true for me. When betrayal paid me a visit, it quickly brought me to my knees. Despair and hopelessness overcame me, and I felt powerless to find a way out. I first confessed this condition to Rozanne.

I was sitting at the desk in my home office, in a pit of devastation, and Rozanne was sitting across from me. I looked her in the eyes as mine began to fill with tears and said, "I think I'm in trouble." It was my way of saying, *I am powerless in the face of this depression; it has me by the throat and I can't do anything about it. I've tried. My life is unmanageable.*

At the time, it felt like the worst place I could possibly be. Looking back, I'm not so sure it was. When I chose to be vulnerable, to openly admit my powerlessness to another, it was my first step out of isolation and into community. It also helped me to acknowledge my powerlessness to God, to admit my need for a Higher Power to heal me and restore me. God is a force that lives above helplessness, a source who can do something about it.

Power over the challenges and evils of this life will not come through self-improvement programs or will-power. The only power that can do anything about the big problems we face in life comes from God alone. The sooner we acknowledge that we are empty, that we are vulnerable and have no power of our own, the better off we will be. Jesus emptied himself of his divine attributes to show us how it's done. Jesus chose powerlessness and then acknowledged it. Unlike Jesus, we don't have to make a choice to be powerless—we *are* powerless, whether we like it or not. But we do get to choose whether or not to *acknowledge* our powerlessness. And one of the ways we do that is to stop trying to pull off the impossible in our own strength. Instead, we should go looking for the power we need from the same source Jesus turned to.

If you assessed yourself at the low end of the empowerment scale, perhaps you're thinking, *Thanks, Randy, but I've already admitted my powerlessness, and I'm still stuck.* If so, I have a question for you. How vulnerable are you in that powerlessness? Is it possible that, just maybe, you are actually *invulnerable* in your powerlessness? That you are living in a state of self-protection and unwilling to even consider the possibility that you or your circumstances could change? To be invulnerable is to be incapable of being wounded or harmed. To be invulnerable in powerlessness is to use powerlessness as protection—to fold your arms, isolate yourself, and erect a fortress around whatever you have left. Self-protection is a natural response to threat, but it's meant to be a temporary measure, not a lifestyle.

If this is where you find yourself, it's okay! The invitation to you is to begin choosing vulnerability. Start as they do in AA meetings. Acknowledge your powerlessness out loud, first to yourself and then to others. Enlist a friend as an accountability partner, and give them permission to challenge you. When you start folding your arms in resignation and make your move to hide under a rock, rely on them to help you step out of your self-protective comfort zone and try something different. And remember, there is a Higher Power you can always lean into for help.

Take a baby step, stick your toe in the water on a smaller issue, and then build on that with more steps until you can tackle the big ones. Before you know it, you will be in a different place, a better place.

Maybe you find yourself uncomfortably sandwiched in the middle of the empowerment scale. Unlike those on the far left of the continuum, who feel hopeless, you may still believe that if you just dig a little deeper or try a little harder, you can pull yourself up by your bootstraps and rise above your challenges. You might repeat mantras such as, *I just need to be more disciplined. I just need a new program. I just need to get my act together.* I hate to be the bearer of bad news, but you can't power up on your powerlessness. Oh, there may be some things you can control and overcome, but we are talking here about the biggies that have your number. I think it is time for a new strategy.

The invitation to you is to consider making a course correction, to humble yourself and admit you can't hold everything together on your own. You face threats—from without or from within—and you are vulnerable to those threats. The world is a dangerous place. All of us who lived through the coronavirus pandemic know that—we were stripped of the illusion that we are actually in control of what happens to us. Denying our vulnerability in the face of a dangerous world will get us nowhere.

Or perhaps you need to admit that the greatest threats you face are internal rather than external. Maybe there are self-defeating habits of thought and behavior that pull you down and keep you "under the circumstances." Daily life runs in a cycle of trying, failing, and beating yourself up for failing—again. No one is making you think or act this way. These are your own self-defeating and self-fulfilling prophecies. Regardless, the invitation is the same—humble yourself and admit you can't tackle whatever it is in your own strength.

Ask yourself, "What might vulnerability require of me?" It doesn't have to be a big thing; it could be a small thing—admitting your powerlessness to God or to a trusted friend. Then ask yourself again, "What does vulnerability require of me *now*?" And keep asking. If you consider yourself to be on the more empowered end of the scale, you can still ask—and keep asking—the same question. Do it now if you're willing.

Years ago, a friend and recovering alcoholic who had earned his thirty-year sobriety coin took me to his weekly AA meeting. While some people there had just begun their journeys and had their guards up, I was blown away by the degree of vulnerability in what most people shared. They were humbly honest about their failures, struggles, and powerlessness, but also full of realistic hope for a better day. I was struck by how powerful their powerlessness was, and it captivated me. When I shared this observation with my host as we were leaving, he responded, "Randy, sometimes I wish all people could be alcoholics so they could go through the steps of recovery." He had experienced the power of being vulnerable in powerlessness and wished everyone could experience it.

Can you believe it? Jesus had power over everything and everyone, but he left it all behind and chose to be vulnerable, to join us in our powerlessness so he could show us the way to an empowered life. The power you need exists. It is real. Take his hand, turn the page, and say yes as he invites you to take your first step into this new way of life.

CHAPTER 2

What We Need to Leave Behind

Rozanne and I have a son named David who was born without a left hand. When David was around five years old, he and I were in the backyard, playing catch with a baseball. To show him how to catch with one hand, I modeled it for him. David threw the ball to me, and I caught it in my glove. Then I tucked the glove under my opposite arm, pulled out the ball, threw it back to him, and put the glove back on again.

Not long after, David's younger brother, Stephen, came out with his glove to play with us. Stephen has both hands, but guess what he did when I threw the ball to him? He caught the ball with his glove, tucked the glove under his opposite arm, pulled out the ball, threw it back to me, and then placed the glove back on again. It never occurred to him that he should do anything other than what he'd seen David and me doing.

It is in our nature to mimic or imitate what we see others doing. In fact, it may be one of the most effective ways we humans learn. "Watch how I do it," then "I'll watch how you do it," is the core of most mentoring relationships. Jesus knew this about us—that we learn by imitation—because he created human beings this way. Therefore, one of the best ways for Jesus to teach us how to overcome our powerlessness was to leave heaven and come down into our backyard and show us how it is done.

As we learned in the previous chapter, Jesus put himself in our shoes when he chose to place himself in our position of powerlessness. In other words, he didn't play catch with two hands, knowing we had only one. He took on our weaknesses and our limitations. He voluntarily stooped to our level to show us how to live. That's what love does.

Paul, the principal leader in spreading the message of Jesus in the first century, most definitely picked up on Jesus' teaching on imitation. In a letter to the believers in Ephesus, Paul gave them this instruction:

Follow God's example, therefore, as dearly loved children. (Ephesians 5:1)

I love how *The Message* puts it:

Watch what God does, and then you do it, like children who learn proper behavior from their parents.

The Greek word Paul used in encouraging us to follow God's example is *mimitai*. It is the root from which we get our word *mimic*. This is actually really good news. Why? Because it means the key to living an empowered life is not rocket science—it isn't out of our reach. We simply have to watch the way Jesus lived and do what he did. Paul not only gave us this priceless piece of guidance; he also took hold of it for himself.

> Follow my example, as I follow the example of Christ.
> (1 Corinthians 11:1)

Here, Paul expanded the prototype to include a team of mentors who have taken Jesus' pattern seriously in their lives. But the original and foundational model is Jesus. We look to his life for our core guidance.

Jesus emptied himself, which means he voluntarily left behind access to his unlimited presence, unlimited knowledge, and unlimited power. This was his first move toward us—and it was a choice to become vulnerable. So, with Jesus as our model, we can make a similar move. We ask ourselves, *What do I need to leave behind? How do I choose vulnerability—especially vulnerability that enables me to experience God's power as Jesus did?*

If we want to experience the resurrection power Jesus did, we, too, must leave something behind. You've probably heard the saying "Nothing changes if nothing changes." If we want to move beyond powerlessness, something has to change—and that almost always requires taking a legitimate risk.

There are an infinite number and variety of risks we might take in choosing vulnerability as Jesus did, but there is one thing every risk requires: giving up *control.*

This is what we need to leave behind. We need to relinquish the control we think we have over our lives and pass it on to the One who actually is in control. Talk about making yourself vulnerable! This was a major theme in Jesus' teaching to the disciples, but there was one occasion in which the setting really helped to drive the point home. When the disciples suddenly found themselves in a position that was beyond their control, they were terrified, as we might be. And yet, Jesus appeared to be surprised or puzzled by their fear. Jesus possessed something the disciples did not, so in classic Jesus style, he asked them questions to help them grow.

"WHY ARE YOU SO AFRAID?"

Jesus had just finished a full day of teaching a large group of people on the shores of the Sea of Galilee. When evening came, he invited his disciples to join him on a boat ride to the other side of the lake. Out of nowhere, a violent storm broke out. Sudden storms were actually quite common on the Sea of Galilee, which is situated in a basin surrounded by mountains. When cool air from the mountains came down through the narrow passes and clashed with the hot, humid air on the lake, it created the perfect conditions for a storm. Waves broke over the boat, filling it with water, and the disciples were understandably terrified that it would capsize at any moment.

Meanwhile, Jesus was in the back of the boat sleeping on a cushion. The disciples had to wake him up, shouting, "Teacher, don't you care if we drown?" (Mark 4:38). Jesus got up and spoke first to the wind and waves, "Quiet! Be still!" (v. 39). Immediately, the storm was over, and everything was calm again.

Then Jesus turned to the disciples and asked two poignant questions: "Why are you so afraid? Do you still have no faith?" (v. 40). The story ends with the disciples being terrified, not at the storm but at what they'd just witnessed with Jesus. They wanted Jesus to care that they were all going to drown, but they had no idea he had the power to bring them back to a place of safety. They turned to each other and asked, "Who is this? Even the wind and the waves obey him!" (v. 41).

For years, I read this story and assumed the reason Jesus wasn't afraid was because he was God and had the power within himself to calm the storm. If I had this ability, a storm wouldn't frighten me either. That's why I always felt somewhat confused by the questions he asked the disciples. They were afraid because they had no control over nature, and Jesus had a unique advantage over the disciples in this way. But when I learned more about Jesus and how he emptied himself of his divine attributes, I realized I was mistaken.

He had emptied himself of omnipresence—he was stuck in that boat with the other disciples. He had emptied himself of omniscience—he didn't even know the storm was coming. He had emptied himself of omnipotence—he had no power of his own to calm the storm. The power required to calm the storm came from the Holy Spirit. In other words, just as the disciples did, Jesus found himself in a situation that was beyond his control. And yet, he had access to power in his powerlessness.

This changes everything about the application of this story. Jesus put himself in a position of defenselessness when he came into our world to represent us. He turned the control of his life over to the Father and the Holy Spirit. He did this voluntarily. Jesus invites his followers to do the same—to give up the illusion that we have control over what happens to us and then to entrust our lives to the only One who is actually stronger than the storms we face. This is what marks the difference between how the disciples responded to the storm and how Jesus did.

Because their faith was in their own limited power, the disciples were terrified when they faced a threat that was more powerful than they were. And yet, the very same circumstances didn't terrify Jesus at all. In fact, the disciples' fear and lack of faith actually surprised Jesus, which is why he asked them, "Why are you so afraid? Do you still have no faith?" (v. 40). He was surprised they were still struggling with something so basic, especially after they had spent so much time with him personally. He wanted his followers to experience the same kind of calm reliance on God he had in the midst of even a violent storm.

Unlike Jesus', our powerlessness is involuntary. So we are not asked to empty ourselves of our power, of which we have only a limited supply. Instead, we are asked to empty ourselves of the illusion of *control*—that exhausting effort of pretending we have power over what happens in our world—so that we can find freedom from worry and access to a power greater than our greatest foes.

OUT OF CONTROL

When the storm of betrayal ravaged my life, the waves crashed over and filled my boat with toxic water. It felt as if fear itself were coursing through my veins and my heart were pounding out of my chest. Eventually, much of what had been my life capsized, and I was left holding on to little more than debris without a life preserver in sight. I had lost control and felt as if I were drowning.

Like the storm on the Sea of Galilee, my storm of betrayal came suddenly and unexpectantly. A few people rocked my boat when they chose to break a promise we'd made to each other years previously. Up to that point in my life, I'd faced the occasional squall, but most were storms I was able to handle in my own strength, or so I thought. However, when I experienced betrayal, I felt as if I were facing off against a Category 5 hurricane with 157-mile-per-hour winds. If there were such a thing as spiritual meteorologists, their forecasts would have included warnings of catastrophic damage: loss of dignity, loss of identity, loss of influence, loss of trust, loss of a dream, loss of income, loss of relationships, loss of hope for the future. I just didn't have the strength to overcome what that storm did to me. It was all I could do to keep my head above water. Eventually, if something didn't change, I knew I would lose the strength to do even that.

The betrayal was the unexpected storm that hit my life, but it actually wasn't what dropped me into a dark season of powerlessness. The root cause of the fear that drove me into a state of anxiety and depression was losing the illusion of control over my circumstances. This was a very important discovery. While I needed to work through the trauma of what had been done to me and eventually forgive those who had trespassed against me, the biggest challenge I faced was being forced to admit I was incapable of controlling my life at all, much less controlling it in my own strength.

When things got unnervingly quiet, particularly at night, I could hear Jesus ask me the same questions he asked the disciples: *Why are you so afraid? Do you still have no faith?* At first, I felt something like embarrassment. At this point in my journey with Jesus, shouldn't I be past something so basic? At the same time, I didn't sense he was angry with me any more than he had been angry at the disciples. Instead, I felt that he loved me deeply and wanted me to live above my fears. For sure, I knew this would not be the last violent storm I would experience, or the last time I would feel powerless over my circumstances. I also knew it was time to take a big risk—to empty myself of the illusion of control and turn control of my life and my circumstances over to God.

For someone like me who is used to being in the driver's seat, it's a huge risk to turn over the wheel to someone else and move to the passenger seat. I had to trust that the One to whom I was surrendering control was capable and trustworthy. What if he fell asleep at the wheel in the middle of my storm? At this point in my journey, I had no way to know what moving to the passenger seat might entail. I had preached many sermons over the years on giving control of one's life to God, and I assumed I had already done this. Apparently, I had not. Was I supposed to just say out loud, "God, I turn the control of my life over to you"? I wasn't sure, but I knew it was time to take a risky next step.

Anytime we experience a storm, we tend to hold on tight with our own strength, trying not to be washed overboard. It requires being on call 24/7 to keep the pieces of our life intact and in place. It is exhausting and, frankly, can't be done. We simply can't bail the water out of our boat fast enough to stay afloat when the storms we face are stronger than us. We can decide to stay in calm waters closer to the shore to prevent any calamity, but what kind of life is that? Why should we be content to settle for the equivalent of being marooned as a castaway on a lonely island when Jesus calls us to venture into deep waters and explore new lands? That is what he did when he chose to relinquish his divine power for our sakes.

Did you know that when someone attempts to rescue a drowning person, the victim's instinct is to fight and struggle instead of relaxing so the rescuer can take over? It's a powerful image, isn't it? If the drowning person fails to take the risk of surrendering control, he cannot be rescued—and he may even take the rescuer down with him.

The struggle to release the illusion of control is a universal problem regardless of where you placed yourself on the empowerment scale. If you assessed yourself on the low side, maybe in the range of 1 to 3, and have an acute awareness of your powerlessness, it doesn't mean you aren't still trying to be the captain of your own boat. You will likely try to stay closer to the shore or maybe avoid ever getting into a boat. You might even isolate yourself on an island away from people or circumstances that can hurt you. However, you will not truly be safe. Not only will you be missing out on God's calling in your life, which is almost always in deeper waters; you will also still be vulnerable to other circumstances beyond your control, perhaps especially the internal struggles that undermine your ability to live in hope and power.

Or, if you happen to feel a little more empowered—in the middle of the empowerment scale—you might courageously venture from the shore and feel you have been more or less "lucky" in life. But there is likely still that sense that, at some point, the proverbial shoe is going to drop out of the sky, someone is going to eventually move your cheese, or a Category 5 storm is going to break out and you will be in the dead middle of it. You might live in silent fear waiting for that day to happen.

Pretty much everyone on the planet got a taste of this in the first several months of the global pandemic of COVID-19. It felt a lot like the storm on the Sea of Galilee—as if it came out of nowhere—and then it spread to every corner of the planet. We hunkered down in our homes for weeks, which turned into months, and we wondered if it wouldn't be years. We lost loved ones and friends, jobs and businesses, homes and retirement accounts. As infection rates skyrocketed and death tolls mounted, few of us doubted that this thing was bigger than us. In fact, for many, myself included, it was the first time when literally the whole world felt out of control.

So, if we can't control what happens to us, what are we supposed to do? The solution is not hunkering down in a hole for the rest of our lives, as appealing as that might seem sometimes. Instead, we need to admit that we are powerless and transfer our faith from ourselves to God. We need to take the risk and leave behind a life in which we try to be in control of things that are simply beyond our control. We need to place ourselves in a vulnerable position, to relax enough and have faith enough to let our Deliverer rescue us. Who knows, we might even get to the place one day where we, too, have the kind of faith that enables us to sleep peacefully through a storm.

TURN OVER CONTROL TO GOD

How do we do that? How do we turn over the control of our lives to God as Jesus did, and as Jesus invites us to do? It's not easy. I sometimes liken it to what trapeze artists do when they have to release their grasp on one bar in order to be caught by a partner swinging from another bar. There is a moment between the release and catch in which they have nothing to hold on to. But they'll never cross from one side to the other if they don't first let go of the bar.

The decision to turn control of our lives over to God—to release our hold on the illusion of control—feels a lot like being suspended in midair. We know we want to get to the other side, where life is better, but we have to let go of the first bar in order to reach out for the next one. When we're stuck in a powerless place, we don't mind change—in fact, we actually long for it. But it's that free-fall transition between letting go and being caught that frightens us. And yet, having taken that flying leap myself, I can say that it is possible—and it is definitely worth the risk.

Even if you don't feel ready to fully let go just yet, there are some steps you can take to keep moving away from fear and toward faith. To help you get started, here are three things I discovered that helped me in my journey.

1. Control What You Can Control

I admit it's a little awkward to start here—to say that the first step in turning over control is to control what you can control—but it is important. God wants us to become vulnerable not to our circumstances but to him. We do that when we admit that our lives are unmanageable. Yet, the truth is that not every area of our lives is unmanageable. There are many things God has given us the capacity and responsibility to manage. We need to make a distinction between the things that are in our control and the things that are not. The need to make this distinction is at the heart of theologian Reinhold Niebuhr's famous Serenity Prayer:

> God, grant me the serenity to accept the things I
> cannot change,
> courage to change the things I can,
> and wisdom to know the difference.

The things I cannot change or control need to be turned over to God. The things God has empowered me to change are the things for which I must take responsibility. Knowing the difference is extremely important.

Sometimes our life is out of control because we are out of control. If we want to move beyond powerlessness, we must first identify and refrain from stirring up avoidable storms. For years, I had a picture in my office of a man with his head bowed and his hands clasped, praying, "Dear Lord, help me meet this self-imposed and totally unnecessary challenge." In other words, we often introduce difficulties into our lives by the choices we make or the things we choose to ignore. In fact, I've come to believe that we can avoid upward of 80 percent of the storms in our lives if we just exercise our legitimate control over some basics.

The book of Proverbs is a great place to start for finding the most basic and commonsense boundaries for our lives. Proverbs calls these boundaries *wisdom* and encourages us to pursue it like lost treasure. In order to secure the benefits of wisdom, we must consistently apply its counsel to our lives. That takes self-control. Listen to the wisdom writer's invitation:

> My child, never forget the things I have
>   taught you.
>   Store my commands in your heart.
> If you do this, you will live many years,
>   and your life will be satisfying.
>   (3:1–2 NLT)

Here's a simple example of what it looks like to exercise this kind of self-control over the basics.

A number of years ago, every time I went to the doctor

or dentist and they checked my blood pressure, it was elevated. I'd never had this problem before, so I thought it must be "white coat syndrome," which is anxiety from being in the doctor's office. I purchased my own blood pressure device to put my mind at ease. When my pressure was still registering high at home, I began to worry and have morbid thoughts: *So, this is how it ends for me?*

When I went to see my doctor for an extensive checkup, he didn't start by writing a prescription for blood pressure medication. Instead, he asked me several questions about my general health and lifestyle, one of which was whether or not I consumed caffeinated drinks. The answer was most definitely yes—a fully loaded, bold Starbucks brew multiple times a day. "Why don't you lay off the caffeine for a while and see what that does?" he suggested. So I did, and my blood pressure immediately went back to normal. I have been off caffeine for over six years now and haven't had a problem with my blood pressure since. All it took was a little—okay, a lot of—self-control.

In the same vein, when I went to that same doctor a few years later to help me overcome my depression, he started out not by focusing on my depression itself but by working through a checklist of healthy disciplines in my life. He wanted to rule out the possibility that the issue was self-induced, just as it had been with my high blood pressure. Keep in mind that at this point I was clinically depressed. Even though I didn't yet have that as an offi-cial diagnosis, I knew my situation was serious. I could have decided to roll my eyes in frustration or even to take offense that the doctor wasn't taking my situation seriously. But I knew he actually was taking my situation seriously by first assessing the basics of a healthy lifestyle, all of which were within my control.

To be clear, I understand that whatever it is that has you feeling powerless is likely complex and potentially serious. I don't mean to diminish that at all. And yet, I wouldn't be serving you well if I didn't at least ask you to take a step back and consider where you're at when it comes to some of the basics—those things that are likely within your control and provide the foundation for a healthy and empowered life. For example:

- getting a good night's sleep
- eating healthy
- exercising
- practicing good personal hygiene
- having strong, healthy relationships
- nurturing your spiritual life
- getting an education
- going to work
- managing your money wisely
- avoiding unhealthy relationships
- avoiding drugs and illegal substances

Not surprisingly, people who practice these things consistently have less drama and trauma in their life.

Now, keep in mind that the focus here is only on the aspects of these things that are legitimately within our control, and not the bigger, more complicated issues outside of our control—specifically, the things that can enter into our lives and make us powerless to perform one or more of the basics. This was certainly true for me.

When I went to my doctor, seeking help with my depression following the betrayal, we assessed a checklist of things within my control, and I did make some adjustments, such as changing my exercise routine. But the root cause of my problem wasn't something I could control—it was bigger than me. I was drifting aimlessly on stormy seas, and controlling the basics alone wouldn't get me back on course. In fact, I actually lost my power to perform some of them, such as getting sufficient sleep and eating well.

I needed something or someone outside of myself to meet me in my powerlessness. I needed an anchor to keep me from continuing to drift aimlessly. Fortunately, finding an anchor was something I'd actually learned about through another brush I'd had with powerlessness several years earlier.

2. Anchor Your Mind in Truth

When our four children were young, we took them on a trip to the Cayman Islands with a number of other families in our neighborhood. On the first day, all the guys decided to take the kids out for the first of many snorkeling adventures. Normally, the waters of the Caymans are smooth and calm, but on this particular day the waters were very rough.

Nevertheless, we all got in the water and started swimming. About thirty yards offshore, I froze. I had this overwhelming sense that we were not safe. As everyone else, including my four children, kept swimming farther out, I felt this urge to swim back to the shore, and yet my children were out there in danger. I literally froze in place. As I did, waves of salt water kept washing over me, making the situation feel even more intense and dangerous by the second.

When I finally began to yell for help, the other guys ignored me. They knew I'd been on the swim team in high school and thought I was joking. When one of the other dads eventually did swim back to where I was, he assured me that everyone was safe and swam back with me to the shore.

Once I was on dry land, I just shook my head. The fear and anguish I'd felt in the water had been completely irrational. We were wearing all the right safety gear, all four of my children could swim, and we were all watching out for each other. Everyone enjoyed another thirty minutes of snorkeling before they returned safely to the shore to meet up with me.

At the time, I tried to shake off the experience as silly. Unfortunately, it didn't shake off as easily as I hoped. Later that night when we were all in bed, I experienced that same overwhelming sensation that my children were in danger. Each time I got up to check on them, they were completely fine. What in the world was going on?

Even after we returned home, I couldn't shake my fear. Trying to reassure myself, I made a bed of blankets on the floor of our bedroom for all my children to sleep on, safe within my sight. Since I let them fall asleep each night watching television, often accompanied by bowls of vanilla ice cream, they had no objections. However, when this went on for six months, I knew it was time to get some help.

With great embarrassment, I shared my dilemma with a Christian counselor. He quickly diagnosed my problem. In simple terms, he said that the experience in the Caymans had essentially reset the computer in my brain to process my circumstances differently. As a result, I could no longer distinguish an authentic threat from an imagined threat—so everything felt threatening. What I needed to do was to reset my mind back to a healthy setting.

He gave me a cassette tape (that's how long ago it was) of a guy with a West Texas accent rehearsing a series of positive statements—specifically, what the Bible says is true about me, about God, and about the world around me. The statements emphasized two things: God's love for me and God's control over my circumstances. Frankly, I thought it was a bit corny, but I promised I would listen to it for thirty minutes twice a day.

Two weeks later, my children were back to sleeping in their rooms again. No one was more shocked than I was. When I had a follow-up meeting with my counselor, I asked him how that worked. "Psychotherapists call it neurolinguistic programming," he said, "but I call it biblical meditation."

The theological schools I attended had cautioned against the practice of meditation, thinking of it as an Eastern religious practice in which people try to empty their minds. And yet, meditation on God's goodness and greatness was a strategy the psalmist often relied on to get him through the difficulties life threw at him.

> "I will remember the deeds of the LORD;
>> yes, I will remember your miracles of long ago.
> I will consider all your works
>> and meditate on all your mighty deeds."
> Your ways, God, are holy.
>> What god is as great as our God?
> (Psalm 77:11–13)

Day and night, the psalmist remembered, considered, and meditated on what he knew to be true about who God is. In so doing, he essentially reset his mind on the truth about his situation in light of his relationship with God. In the New Testament, Paul described this as the "renewing of [the] mind" (Romans 12:2). Meditating on biblical truth is an anchor that gives us stability in the midst of the storms life throws our way.

During my crisis of betrayal, one of the things I did every morning for about three months straight was to sit with a psalm for an hour. First, I listened to the psalm several times on audio while simultaneously reading along with it in my Bible. Then I finished by writing a prayer in my journal, rehearsing the truths I'd just heard.

Anchoring my mind in biblical truth through meditation didn't dispatch my depression in two weeks as it had my irrational fears after the episode in the Caymans. But slowly and eventually, it did drop a heavy anchor that steadied me and helped me reset my mind on the truth that God was bigger than this storm. It was a small step away from fear and toward faith, one that helped me keep moving toward God in trust and vulnerability.

3. Transfer Control—Officially

We must surrender the illusion of control, but we can't stop there. We must take one more step to turn control over to God, who can handle whatever it is we're facing, no problem. And this isn't something we do just once or even occasionally. It's a discipline we need to practice daily, sometimes from one moment to the next.

Here is what I find helpful for my soul and sanity when I need to surrender control to God. I make the transfer of responsibility official with three simple movements in prayer.

- I clinch my fists as tightly as I can. Then I share openly with God the fear, the tension, the worry, and the anxiety I am experiencing. I lay my requests before him as honestly as I can, as he has asked us to (Philippians 4:6–7). With every request, I squeeze my fists a little tighter. The tension runs up my arms as my body connects with the brokenness in my spirit.

- I turn my palms upward and open them fully. I release the tension I have been holding and acknowledge my inability to deal with whatever I am facing in my own power. I take a deep breath and whisper to God, "I am powerless to handle this on my own. I desperately need your help!"

- I turn my open hands over, palms facing down. This symbolizes that I am letting go of all I have been holding on to. I have turned it over to God in faith. Then I whisper, "I am trusting in you and you alone to see me through this." I sit quietly, breathing deeply in and out and inviting the Spirit to confirm in my spirit that I am a child of God and that he's got me (Romans 8:14–17, 26–27).

It is a simple exercise, yet it has been profoundly helpful in training my mind and heart to turn away from fear and toward faith, to allow God to be God, and to live in the power that comes from trusting that he really is in control.

"HOW CAN YOU BE SO CALM?"

Jesus chose powerlessness. He put himself in a vulnerable place and position for our sakes. He did this to show us how to leave behind our powerlessness so we can live in his mighty strength. If we want to overcome our fears and live in that power—to have the faith that enabled Jesus to be calm in the middle of a storm—we must do what Jesus did. We must put ourselves in a vulnerable place, admit our powerlessness, and leave behind the illusion that we are in control of our lives. Instead of giving up power, as Jesus did, we must come to terms with the fact that we are born limited.

As someone who has experienced life on both ends of the empowerment scale, I can tell you one thing I know for sure. No matter where you are, the act of surrender is not nearly as bad as it sounds. Truth is, trying to be God is no cakewalk. It is exhausting to wake up every day believing you have to be able to handle anything and everything that comes your way. I know because I lived that way and felt that way for most of my life. Then real life hit me. If it hasn't hit you yet, trust me: it will. It doesn't matter how smart you are, how much money you have, or how strong you feel; there's a storm out there with your name on it. Take it from Solomon, the wisest man who ever lived:

The race is not to the swift or the battle to the strong,
nor does food come to the wise or wealth to the

brilliant or favor to the learned; *but time and chance happen to them all.* (Ecclesiastes 9:11, emphasis added)

Don't wait until chance takes you out. Start surrendering now. That's my best advice.

The longer we insist on living with the illusion of control, the more vulnerable we are to the undertow of difficult circumstances. When an unexpected storm breaks out that is clearly bigger and stronger than us, we'll have little to turn to but our own fear. And take it from me: that is not a place you want to be.

I was a self-professed "empowered person" when I experienced betrayal, and yet I responded just as the disciples did when the storm threatened to capsize their boat. I was terrified. I felt immobilized. And there was no question that my life was out of control. I knew I needed to anchor my life in truth and consciously turn over control to God.

How do we know if we have emptied ourselves as Jesus did? Well, for starters, I can tell you that it isn't a onetime event but a way of life. Every day, we have an unlimited number of opportunities to surrender ourselves in faith, to empty ourselves of the illusion of control, to refuse to play God—and to do it all so we can be filled with the One who is all-powerful. Not a bad trade.

Surrendering control won't change your life overnight. At least it didn't for me. But over time, I began to feel a shift in my soul. Buds of hope appeared on the branches of my life. I started to envision a day when people no longer asked me, "Why are you so afraid?"— which many people did—but asked instead, "How can you be so calm in the middle of this storm?"

PART II

Aligned

CHAPTER 3

How Jesus Lived

There was a little girl who was being unruly, disobedient, and obstinate. Exasperated, her mother finally told her to sit in the corner until her attitude changed. The little girl, with arms folded, stomped over to a small chair in the corner and sat down. A few minutes later, she shouted out, "Mom, I may be sitting down on the outside, but I'm standing up on the inside!"

Maybe you can relate. I know I can.

I went to school in the days when teachers could use their rulers to slap our open palms as a warning: *Get your act together—or else!* That actually happened to me back in my elementary school days. Keep in mind, this was the 1960s. I stopped misbehaving on the outside to prevent another ruler slapping in front of my peers, but I was no less obstinate on the inside.

Unfortunately, whatever it is about human nature that causes us to buck authority as children doesn't go away when we become adults. We just develop more sophisticated ways of sitting down on the outside while standing up on the inside. And it's a dynamic that plays out in every area of life, including our spiritual life.

One of the most common examples of this is the "Sunday Christian." If I'm a Sunday Christian, I "sit down" in church on Sunday, but "stand up" in my Monday-through-Saturday life. I comply with expectations in church, but often act very differently outside of church. I might recite the Lord's Prayer on Sunday, forgiving those who have trespassed against me, but on the inside still hold a grudge toward the one who hurt me. I might shout "Amen!" when the pastor preaches about loving our neighbors as ourselves, but then post a scathing rant on Facebook about my neighbor for having different views than I do.

Sitting down on the inside is hard. There is something in our nature that makes us want to do the opposite of God's instructions. The apostle Paul described this dynamic in his own life when he wrote:

> For I do not do the good I want to do, but the evil I do not want to do—this I keep on doing. (Romans 7:19)

And yet this is not the dynamic that plays out in the relationship Jesus had with the Father. Instead, Jesus constantly sought to align his life—inside and out—with his Father's will. He didn't do this out of obligation or to avoid punishment, but out of desire—it was his passion to please the Father and to rely on the Holy Spirit's power to achieve his mission on earth. He *wanted* to sit down on the inside, to always be surrendered to the Father. He trusted in the good plan of the Father, and he wanted to align his life with it—for his own sake, but mostly for our sakes. He wanted to show us that living *aligned* is living for something better and greater than ourselves. And he wanted us to learn how to trust that God's plan for us is good and for our good, even when we don't understand it at the time.

So what exactly does it mean to sit down on the inside? In a word, it means *surrender.* A surrender of the will that allows us to align our lives, inside and out, with the will of the Father. It means we wave the white flag, not as a declaration of defeat, but as a declaration of desire—a sign that we are ready and willing to take the next step into a life of true empowerment. And once again, Jesus shows us how.

JESUS DESIRED THE WILL OF THE FATHER

Jesus had a will of his own, but he freely submitted his will to the will of the Father. From one moment to the next, he aligned his entire life—everything he said and did—with God's will. On the one hand, that might not sound like anything new. Of course he was aligned with God's will, right? And yet, even as a pastor who has spent nearly three decades studying and teaching Scripture, I have to admit that I was actually stunned when I examined this more closely.

I hadn't fully understood how determined Jesus was to align his will with the will of the Father until I put together many stories from his life and studied them side by side. And so I'd like to take you on a similar journey through the life of Christ to show you what I discovered. To do that, we're going to consider several examples, so I need you to hang in there with me. While I don't want to overwhelm you, I do want you to see this undeniable pattern in the life of Jesus. It reveals just how important it is for you and for me to learn to sit down on the inside in order to live an empowered life.

When Jesus was a boy, he and his parents joined with a large group of friends and relatives and headed to Jerusalem to celebrate Passover, the most important festival on the Jewish calendar. Afterward, they were on their way home when they discovered Jesus wasn't with them. They returned to Jerusalem and finally located him three days later. They found him in the temple courts, sitting with the teachers, listening to them and asking them questions. When his parents expressed their anxiety and questioned him, this was his answer:

> Why did you seek Me? Did you not know that I must be about My Father's business? (Luke 2:49 NKJV)

Even in this early stage of his life, Jesus was consumed with the will of the Father. It was his Father's will that drove everything. Again, not out of fear or obligation but out of a passion to know more about God and God's good plan for his life. Jesus didn't just wait around and hope that God's will would somehow walk by. He sought it out and then followed it with enthusiasm. Luke ended the story declaring, "Jesus grew in wisdom and in stature and in favor with God and all the people" (v. 52 NLT). When Jesus, as equal with the Father, left the heavens to come walk among us and represent us to the Father, he left behind his full knowledge as God. As a result, we find him in the temple asking questions, saturating his mind in the Word of God, soaking it in and growing daily in wisdom.

Once he became a man, Jesus fully engaged in his God-ordained purpose. On one particularly hot day in the region of Samaria, Jesus had a compelling conversation with a woman at a well. When his disciples returned from a grocery run and urged him to eat something, Jesus responded, "I have food to eat that you know nothing about" (John 4:32). Naturally, they concluded someone must have given him food before they arrived. Supernaturally, Jesus stated, "My food . . . is to do the will of him who sent me and to finish his work" (v. 34). He declared that his very life was sustained by doing God's will. In other words, taking in the will of the Father satisfied Jesus' spirit much as a full plate of favorite foods satisfies the body.

Later, Jesus was in Jerusalem on the Sabbath and healed a guy who had been an invalid for thirty-eight years. Naturally, this caught the attention of everyone in the town, including the Jewish leaders, who had a big problem with what Jesus had done.

So, because Jesus was doing these things on the Sabbath, the Jewish leaders began to persecute him. In his defense Jesus said to them, "My Father is always at his work to this very day, and I too am working." For this reason they tried all the more to kill him; not only was he breaking the Sabbath, but he was even calling God his own Father, making himself equal with God. (John 5:16–18)

Old Testament law forbade anyone from working on the Sabbath, which started at sundown on Friday night and went through sundown on Saturday. The act of healing was considered work. But the Jewish leaders had an even bigger problem when Jesus referred to God as his Father. In that time and culture, such a personal, intimate reference was essentially a claim of being equal with God. News alert—Jesus *is* equal with God! He chose not to take advantage of his divine position while he walked the earth, but he was no less God in his very nature.

Jesus gave the religious leaders this answer:

Very truly I tell you, the Son can do nothing by himself; he can do only what he sees his Father doing, because whatever the Father does the Son also does. For the Father loves the Son and shows him all he does. Yes, and he will show him even greater works than these, so that you will be amazed. (vv. 19–20)

Jesus did only what the Father did and only what the Father told him to do. He even said he could do nothing by himself. Jesus placed himself in utter dependence on the will of the Father. If the Father didn't move or speak, Jesus didn't move or speak. *Wow!* Feeling a little amazed yet? Me too! I have never met anyone who gets so much joy out of submitting to the will of another person. We need to keep pressing on, because it is the full extent to which Jesus goes with his surrendered will that opens the door to power. Take a deep breath and keep reading. Jesus is leading us to a very good place.

The day after Jesus miraculously fed more than five thousand people with just five loaves and two fish, the people tracked him down on the other side of the lake in hopes of receiving another "Happy Meal." Jesus told them:

> For I have come down from heaven not to do my will but to do the will of him who sent me. (John 6:38)

When Jesus said he had come down from heaven, he was signaling that he was God, yet he didn't act from his own will. Rather, Jesus did only what God the Father wanted him to do. It would have been easy for Jesus to want to fudge just a little here to keep his approval ratings rising, as many of us might do. But not Jesus. He wanted only the applause of the Father.

On another occasion, Jesus was teaching in the temple

courts and once again got pushback from religious leaders. At one point, Jesus said to them:

> You are from below; I am from above. You are of this
> world; I am not of this world. (John 8:23)

Here, Jesus once again clearly claimed he was God.
Then he said:

> When you have lifted up the Son of Man, then you
> will know that I am he and that I do nothing on my
> own but speak just what the Father has taught me.
> (v. 28)

Here, Jesus stated that God the Father was actually
teaching him. Jesus was learning from the Father and then
teaching what he learned to others. You see the pattern,
right? Jesus was passionate about aligning his life with
the will of the Father in all things. But Jesus didn't enter
this world knowing the full game plan. I want this to
make such an impression on you that you can't help but
be amazed at what you see in Jesus' life: he never lets up
on pursuing the will of the Father. Lean in with me as we
continue walking with Jesus.

Later, Jesus was with his disciples when they came
upon a man who had been blind from birth. The disciples
assumed that the man was blind because either he or his
parents had sinned. Jesus told them:

> Neither this man nor his parents sinned . . . but this
> happened so that the works of God might be displayed
> in him. As long as it is day, we must do the works of
> him who sent me. (John 9:3–4)

Once again, Jesus declared that his every waking moment was devoted to doing the works or the will of the One who sent him—the Father. When Jesus said, "As long as it is day," he was conveying a sense of urgency, that there is no time to waste when it comes to doing God's will. And did you notice how Jesus also used the word "we"? It is not just Jesus who should be passionate about accomplishing the Father's mission; *we* need to join in it. In this case, it was the will of the Father for this man to be healed, so Jesus spat on the ground, made some mud, smeared it on the blind man's eyes, and told him to go wash it off in a nearby pool. The guy did so and was healed instantly. The will of the Father was accomplished.

Jesus had another hostile encounter with the Jewish leaders while at the temple in Jerusalem. They wanted to know his identity. When he identified himself as the Messiah, they considered it blasphemy and picked up stones to kill him. Again, Jesus knew and declared publicly that he was equal with God. This was never in question. Before they could throw their stones, Jesus said to them:

> Do not believe me unless I do the works of my Father.
> But if I do them, even though you do not believe me,

believe the works, that you may know and understand
that the Father is in me, and I in the Father. (John
10:37–38)

Remember, even though Jesus was God, he had chosen not to use this to his own advantage. Instead, he made
it his mission to discover what the Father wanted him to
do and then he did it. In this encounter, Jesus said his
identity could be discovered by looking at the sum of his
works. It's a statement that raises a question we might all
ask ourselves: *Who would people say I am by looking at
my works?* Jesus was convinced the message of his works
would lead people to the conclusion he was who he said
he was—the Messiah.

As Jesus came to the end of his public ministry, ten-
sions with the religious leaders continued to rise. Jesus
clarified again that he wasn't acting on his own authority
or his own wisdom.

For I did not speak on my own, but the Father who
sent me commanded me to say all that I have spoken. I
know that his command leads to eternal life. So whatever I say is just what the Father has told me to say.
(John 12:49–50)

Jesus attributed the very words he spoke to instructions he received from the Father. God the Father
"commanded" him, "told" him what to say. Jesus gladly

complied. At no point did Jesus resent the authority of the Father, as we sometimes do with those in authority over us. He knew the Father's purposes were good.

In Jesus' famous "vine and branches" message, he said, "If you keep my commands, you will remain in my love, just as I have kept my Father's commands and remain in his love" (John 15:10). Jesus led his life, got his marching orders, and planned his days around what the Father wanted him to do. His pattern was consistent and constant. Jesus was passionate about and preoccupied with discovering and doing the will of the Father. But did you catch the really important connection he made here? He didn't talk only about receiving the Father's commands; he also talked about receiving the Father's love. For Jesus, obedience and love walked hand in hand. Obedience to the good plans of his Father kept Jesus within the flow of the Father's love. Jesus knew the arrangement was not just one of compliance (sitting down on the outside) but one of alliance (sitting down on the inside), so that he could be exactly where he wanted to be—in the flow of the Father's great love. For Jesus, to be in alignment was to be in love.

John recorded a beautiful and intimate prayer Jesus prayed to the Father near the end of his ministry. In it, Jesus declared his alliance with these words: "I have brought you glory on earth by finishing the work you gave me to do" (17:4). Jesus didn't do the work *he* had determined to do, but only the work the Father gave him to do.

This was the plan from the very beginning. The writer

of Hebrews quoted Jesus, as Jesus himself quoted portions of Psalm 40, in stating the purpose for which he came:

> Therefore, when Christ came into the world,
>   he said:
>   "Here I am—it is written about me in the
>   scroll—
>   I have come to do your will, my God."
>   (Hebrews 10:5, 7)

Jesus' way of being in the world, his modus operandi, was always clear. From the moment he was born, his eyes were fixed on doing nothing more and nothing less than fulfilling the will of his Father, even to the point of death. This is not something Jesus merely said or even decided on his own—it was written in the prophetic scrolls that foretold of the Messiah's mission.

Perhaps no event in the life of Jesus more powerfully demonstrates the radical nature of his dependence on God and his obedience to God's will than the prayer he offered up in the Garden of Gethsemane on the night before his crucifixion. Jesus, like everyone else living during the Roman Empire, knew full well the brutality that was execution by crucifixion. The drawn-out process would be utterly humiliating and excruciating. Jesus knew that he would feel, as any human being would, the full force of degradation and pain, trauma and betrayal, injustice and hopelessness. As a human, he was anxious. He told his disciples before he entered the interior of the garden, "My soul is overwhelmed with sorrow to the point of death" (Matthew 26:38).

Once Jesus was by himself, he fell face to the ground and prayed:

My Father! If it is possible, let this cup of suffering be taken away from me. Yet I want your will to be done, not mine. (Matthew 26:39 NLT)

He prayed this prayer not just once, but three times.

Jesus pleaded for a stay of execution. Could anyone blame him? Surely, by this time he knew there was no other way for salvation to be made available to the entire human race. He was the spotless lamb, the Messiah about whom the Old Testament prophets wrote. He was the sinless Son of God. He had not cratered to any temptation. This was the only possible solution. If not Jesus, then who? If not Jesus, then humanity would be without hope. Yet Jesus petitioned the Father to see if there might be another way.

Jesus finished all three prayers with a declaration that had been true throughout his entire thirty-three years walking this earth. He surrendered himself to his Father: "Yet not as I will, but as you will." This is the climax, the crescendo of Jesus' life purpose. The gospel texts don't record the Father's answer, but Jesus' actions make it clear that he understood the Father's will.

Then he returned to the disciples and said to them,
"Are you still sleeping and resting? Look, the hour has
come, and the Son of Man is delivered into the hands
of sinners. Rise! Let us go! Here comes my betrayer!"
(Matthew 26:45–46)

You can sense the resolve in Jesus' voice. He had
received a clear answer. It was the Father's will for Jesus
to face the cross for the love of humankind. "Rise," he
said. "Let us go!" Jesus was saying, "I know without a
doubt what I am to do. There is no turning back. Let's
get this done!" That is a picture of total surrender to the
will of the Father. Of course, we all know how this story
turned out. Three days later, Jesus was alive again and the
path had been laid for all people to come into an eternal
relationship with God.

OUR SURRENDER

Looking at the life of Jesus and his passion to align his
every moment with the will of his Father made me reflect
on my own situation. Jesus had already shown me that I
could start to overcome the storm of betrayal by turning
over the control of my life to God. Daily emptying myself
of the false sense that I was in control and anchoring my
trust in God seemed to stabilize my life a bit. My next step
toward tapping into the power Jesus possessed required

surrendering my will to the will of the Father. What might this look like? Where might it take me next? Was I up for the adventure?

I knew I needed to shift my focus from the betrayal to God's greater mission for my life, but it was proving to be quite difficult. Then I realized that Jesus himself had a betrayer—in fact, that is the word he used for Judas in the Garden of Gethsemane (Matthew 26:46). Judas betrayed Jesus to the religious leaders for thirty pieces of silver (vv. 14–16). Jesus must have been crushed by this act against him.

I had no problem entering into this part of Jesus' story. I actually felt even closer to him because of it. But I was also aware of the profound contrast between how Jesus dealt with his betrayal and how I'd dealt with mine. Jesus' betrayal didn't sideline him as my betrayal had sidelined me. Whereas I felt immobilized and powerless, Jesus seemed determined and empowered. What was the catalyst for Jesus' determination and ability to keep moving forward? We can't know for certain, but I think at least part of it is because Jesus lived in an intimate and surrendered relationship with the Father. He understood that the Father's plan was bigger—he trusted that even Judas's evil actions could be used by God to accomplish redemption. We now know he was absolutely correct.

I wanted to believe that God's plan for me was bigger than the betrayal, but I still struggled. How could I take on the surrendered mindset of Christ? How could

I do whatever it was I needed to do to move myself forward from self-pity to purpose, and then from purpose to power? The one thing I knew for certain was that I couldn't do anything on my own, so I reached out to two friends. One was a retired engineer and the other a retired geologist. Both had an ability to cut through emotions, which was a struggle for me at the time. Both were extremely methodical and logical in the way they made decisions, sort of cut-and-dried, which I needed to help me see through the fog of my depression. And both men saw something completely different in the betrayal than I did. Instead of seeing it as a dead end, they saw it as a catalyst to something new. You might think that encouraged me, but it actually bothered me that they weren't more sympathetic to my pity party. Even so, I kept listening.

Because the betrayal had caused me to question whether or not I still had a career in ministry, both men gave me a simple and basic assignment. I was to draw a line down the middle of a page to create two columns—one for pros and one for cons—and start listing the pros and cons of the different ministry options I had before me. Then I was to assign a value to each option based on the answer to this question: "Where might I have the greatest impact for God's kingdom?" That was their driving inquiry. For my two friends, discerning God's will for me was a simple mathematical formula. On the one hand, it seemed a bit cold and calculated, but on the other, it definitely helped me shift my focus from myself to God's will.

Before I had any sense of where this exercise might take me, I decided to stick my toe in the pool of surrendered obedience. It was by no means easy. The initial chill made me wonder what full immersion might feel like. In the early days of my depression especially, I struggled to believe I had anything valuable left in me. I thought my best years were behind me, or that whatever God might have in mind for me wouldn't be all that fun. I wondered how surrendered I could be if God's will required something of me I really didn't care for at all. And it's not like there wasn't precedent for that—certainly, the cross wasn't something Jesus looked forward to. Self-doubt often continued to cloud my judgment and made it harder for me to see beyond the betrayal to God's bigger plan.

I did eventually get there, and I'll share more about that in the chapters to come. But for now, I want you to consider your own life and situation. Your story is likely very different from mine, but chances are that we have been in the same place—that place of feeling powerless and not in control.

If you're willing to take the next step to tap into God's mighty strength, you can choose to do what Jesus did. You can surrender your will and align your life with the will of God. You can choose to not only sit down on the outside, but willingly sit down on the inside—and with the same passion Jesus did. You can move from compliance to alliance. What that requires and how that plays out will be different for you than it was—and is—for me.

But perhaps one of the best places to start is to imagine how your life might be different if you were aligned, inside and out, with the will of the Father as Jesus was.

How might your life be different if . . .

- you didn't wait around and hope that God's will would somehow appear but actively sought it out?
- you considered surrender to God a declaration of desire rather than of defeat?
- you could experience doing God's will to be as satisfying as eating a plate of your favorite foods?
- you cared only about the applause from God?
- you acted on God's will with a sense of urgency rather than reluctance or resistance?
- you considered obedience not as compliance but as alliance—a choice to remain in the flow of God's love?
- you were willing to entrust not only your life to God but also your death to God, believing his plan is ultimately a good plan?

If you're anything like me, questions such as these might stir up a mix of both hope and discouragement. You want the life you imagine you might have, and yet you're all too aware of the ways you've failed in the past, the obstacles you face in the present, or the impossibilities you anticipate in the future. Hear me when I say, I know. I feel you. This is hard.

It's hard in part because imagining how your life could be different requires hope. Hope is always risky—especially when it requires surrender. And yet, a surrendered will was one of the most significant components of Jesus' access to power. That's what the pattern of his life and his teaching so clearly reveals.

Might I encourage you to sit down—inside and outside—by whispering a white-flag prayer of "yes" to God? Not out of fear that God is going to zap you or love you less if you don't, but out of a belief that he loves you and wants the best for you. The status quo of your powerlessness will still be there waiting for you if you want to go back to it later, right? So why not try something different and see if it takes you to a new place, a better place? Come with me as we turn the page and discover together how we get there.

CHAPTER 4

How We Need to Live

The greatest tightrope walker in history was a Frenchman named Charles Blondin. In 1859, with large crowds looking on, he stretched out an 1,100-foot rope across the raging waters of Niagara Falls and walked across it from the American side to the Canadian side.[1] The crowds erupted in applause. Then he did it again and again, each time adding a new twist. He did it blindfolded, on stilts, with a sack over his head, and even riding a bicycle. On another occasion, he did somersaults and backflips across the 3.25-inch diameter rope. One time, he carried out a working stove, sat down halfway across, and cooked an omelet. He then lowered the meal down to passengers in a cruise boat 160 feet beneath him. The average walk across and back took twenty-three nail-biting minutes.

One day, Blondin walked across pushing a wheelbarrow. When he got to the other side, he reportedly said, "How many of you believe I can put a person in this wheelbarrow and push them across the tightrope?" Everybody cheered their belief that he could do it. But when he asked for a volunteer, there was silence. No one raised their hand.[2] It is one thing to say you believe in something; it is another thing altogether to actually act on that belief. Until you take action, there is no power in your belief.

Jesus offers us an invitation similar to the one Blondin offered the crowd—to express our faith in action. As we learned in the previous chapter, Jesus aligned his life with the will of his Father. It was his number one passion. And he invites us to make it our passion as well. "Come, follow me," he calls out to us (Matthew 4:19).

What exactly does it mean to make God's will our passion? We got a key piece of insight into that when the disciples asked Jesus to teach them how to pray. Jesus responded with what we now refer to as the Lord's Prayer:

"This, then, is how you should pray:

"'Our Father in heaven,
hallowed be your name,
your kingdom come,
your will be done,
    on earth as it is in heaven.
Give us today our daily bread.
And forgive us our debts,
    as we also have forgiven our debtors.
And lead us not into temptation
    but deliver us from the evil one.'"
(Matthew 6:9–13)

Did you catch the key insight? It comes in the phrase "your will be done, *on earth as it is in heaven.*" That was Jesus' passion—for God's will to reign on earth—and he wanted everything he did and said to be aligned with that mission. That was what gave him access to extraordinary power.

The power of God for our lives is found in doing the will of God in our lives. We can't skirt this requirement or settle for anything less than "your will be done" if we want to tap into the same power that raised Jesus from the dead. But neither can we ignore the fact that it's a bit scary to step out over the deep waters of surrender onto a narrow rope of faith when you already feel overwhelmed and frightened on solid ground. At least, that was how I felt.

When betrayal and depression took me out, my initial instincts were to curl up in a ball and protect what was left of my self-esteem and dignity. Although self-protection is a natural response to threat, over time it became clear to me that self-protection would not get me back on my feet. I had known and taught for many years that it is often in the midst of our most difficult seasons that God calls us to our greatest adventures. I trusted that this might be true for me, but I couldn't take the necessary risks to align myself with God's will if I didn't know what it was. *What is God's will for me now? How do I hear God's voice?* It's an essential question all of us face when we want to move beyond powerlessness.

HEARING GOD'S VOICE

I had the privilege of being mentored by a wonderful follower of Jesus named Dallas Willard.[3] I listened intently to everything he said to me personally and immersed myself in his writings. His book *Hearing God* profoundly influenced my understanding of how to listen for and recognize the voice of God. Dallas himself had been influenced by a British pastor and author named Frederick B. Meyer. Dallas wrote:

> If I could keep only one bit of writing on hearing God outside of the Bible itself, it would be hard to pass over a few pages from Frederick B. Meyer's book, *The Secret of Guidance*.[4]

A recommendation like that from Dallas was all I needed to dive into Meyer's book. Meyer highlighted three "witnesses" or "lights" we can consult in determining what God wants us to do. The three witnesses are the Word, the Spirit, and circumstances. Let's take a closer look and consider how each one gets us closer to hearing God's will for us.

The Word

F. B. Meyer wrote, "The Word is the wire along which the voice of God will certainly come to you if the heart is hushed and the attention fixed."[5] Dallas Willard reinforced this thought when he wrote:

> Each way God communicates with us has its own special uses, but all the ways are not equally significant for our life with him. In terms of overall importance, the written Word and Jesus, the living Word, aren't to be compared to a voice or vision used by God to speak to an individual.[6]

Both spiritual giants told us that God's Word is the foundational source for hearing God and knowing his will. This pattern is clearly evident in the life of Jesus. Perhaps the most vivid example is when Jesus was tempted by Satan.

Immediately following Jesus' baptism, the Spirit led him into the desert, where he fasted for forty days (Matthew 4:1–2). At the end of this time, his body was beaten down and weak. Remember, too, that Jesus had emptied himself of his full knowledge and full power. He was in an extremely vulnerable position when Satan posed three temptations:

> If you are the Son of God, tell these stones to become bread. (v. 3)

> If you are the Son of God . . . throw yourself down. (v. 6)

All this I will give you . . . if you will bow down and worship me. (v. 9)

Jesus responded to each temptation by quoting Scripture:

No! The Scriptures say, "People do not live by bread alone, but by every word that comes from the mouth of God." (v. 4 NLT, quoting Deuteronomy 8:3)

It is also written: "Do not put the Lord your God to the test." (v. 7, quoting Deuteronomy 6:16)

Away from me, Satan! For it is written: "Worship the Lord your God, and serve him only." (v. 10, quoting Deuteronomy 6:13)

Notice what Jesus *didn't* do when he was tempted: he didn't stop to pray. He didn't have to pray for guidance to discern what God would have him do, because God's good and perfect will had already been revealed in the Scriptures. Jesus knew the Word, trusted the Word, and deployed the Word. As a result, he had power to defeat his archenemy. That same source of guidance and power is available to us.

There is no substitute for learning God's Word, as Jesus did. "I have hidden your word in my heart," wrote the psalmist, "that I might not sin against you"

(Psalm 119:11). We do the same when we hide the Word in our hearts to align ourselves with God's will. When we consistently immerse ourselves in the truths of Scripture, we slowly internalize key biblical principles we can rely on to guide our lives according to God's will. Then, when we need guidance and God's Word is clear, we have the confidence we need to trust it and act on it.

The Spirit

The second way F. B. Meyer said we can hear God's voice is directly from the Spirit, who resides within every follower of Jesus. The Bible also refers to this as God's "still small voice" (1 Kings 19:12 NKJV). Dallas Willard wrote:

> The still, small voice—or the interior or inner voice, as it is also called—is the preferred and most valuable form of individual communication for God's purposes. . . . This, I believe, is the primary *subjective* way that God addresses us. Of all the ways in which a message comes from *within* the experience of the person addressed (such as dreams and visions and other mental states), the form of one's own thoughts and attendant feelings is the most common path for hearing God for those who are living in harmony with God.[7]

In a nutshell, there are times when God's Spirit speaks directly to our spirits. God's voice bypasses our flesh and minds, where things get distorted, and speaks directly to the deepest part of us—our spirits. It is the purest form of communication. Pay careful attention to what Paul wrote about this in his first letter to the believers at Corinth:

> The Spirit searches all things, even the deep things of God. For who knows a person's thoughts except their own spirit within them? In the same way no one knows the thoughts of God except the Spirit of God. What we have received is not the spirit of the world, but the Spirit who is from God, so that we may understand what God has freely given us. (1 Corinthians 2:10–12)

Note that last line. We have been given the Spirit "so that we may understand what God has freely given us." God is not trying to hide his will from us. We don't have to have a special magnifying glass or a decoder ring to figure it out. He wants us to know his will so we can experience the best he has for us. The Spirit has been given to us to help us receive God's will and to empower us to follow it.

In Paul's letter to the Christians in Rome, he described how the Spirit communicates as an intermediary: the Spirit speaks to our spirit, and the Spirit speaks to God on our behalf. He wrote, "The Spirit himself testifies with our spirit that we are God's children" (Romans 8:16). The Spirit speaks *to us*. Just a few paragraphs later, he wrote, "The Spirit intercedes for God's people in accordance with the will of God" (v. 27). The Spirit speaks *for us*. When we are weak and do not know how to pray, Paul wrote, "the Spirit himself intercedes for us through wordless groans" (v. 26). The Spirit's prayers, shaped in accordance with God's will, go straight to the Father, which is key to unlocking the power of God in our lives.

So how do we attend to the still, small voice of the Spirit? We follow the apostle Paul's admonition to "pray without ceasing" (1 Thessalonians 5:17 NASB). Now, before you write that off as impossible, hear me out. I am one of those people who has always struggled to pray, and this admonition buried me in a pile of guilt for a long time. Then I realized that prayer isn't fundamentally bowing my head and rattling off a list of prayer requests for an hour. Prayer is primarily a conversation with God in which I seek to hear more from him than he hears from me. So, several years ago, I started turning the endless conversation I was having with myself all day long into an ongoing conversation with God instead.

God, I am going into a difficult meeting today. What should be my frame of mind, my priority? What do I need to say? What should I not say? Then I sit still and listen.

God, I have a mass on my thyroid being biopsied tomorrow. I am scared. Can you give me the right perspective? You tell me not to worry about anything. Any insights on how I can pull this off? Then I sit still and listen.

God, I'm feeling a bit stuck these days. I don't see

many things in my life working right now. I'm actually feeling depressed and like a failure. What do you think is going on here? What do you think about me? What do you want me to do or not do? Then I sit still and listen.

I often use my journal to have this dialogue with God and to write what I feel my spirit is hearing. I find this practice of praying without ceasing calms me down and stills my soul to hear the whispers of the Spirit. How do I know it is the voice of God and not just the voice of my subconscious? Twentieth-century American missionary E. Stanley Jones has one of the best responses to that question that I know of. He wrote:

> Perhaps the rough distinction is this: The voice of the subconscious argues with you, tries to convince you; but the inner voice of God does not argue, does not try to convince you. It just speaks and it is self-authenticating. It has the feel of the voice of God within it.[8]

God is not a bully trying to overpower us and force us to do what he wants. His whisper is gentle, wooing us in the direction of what is good and right. The more we sit still to listen, the easier it is to hear. Willard commented on this when he wrote:

> When our lives are devoted to the will of God, he has reason to speak to us. . . . With assistance from those

who understand the divine voice from their own experience and with an openness and will to learn on our part, we can come to recognize the voice of God without great difficulty.[9]

Confession time. Although I have been studying the Bible since I was fourteen, the churches and institutions I attended in my formative years shied away from, or at least overlooked, this teaching on the Spirit's gentle whisper. I think they distrusted the crazy claims people sometimes made when they said things such as, "God told me . . ." I understand and support the caution. And yet, it also cuts us off from a significant source of God's guidance and power. As I learned more over the years, and as I was mentored by Dallas Willard, I discovered that listening to God's still, small voice within not only provided great comfort, healing, and direction, but also put fresh wind into the sails of my spiritual life. God has never felt more present or real to me than when the Spirit speaks directly to my spirit.

Be still and listen . . . He is trying to tell you something.

Circumstances

The third witness espoused by F. B. Meyer to help us hear God's will is "circumstances." Meyer wrote:

The circumstances of our daily life are to us an infallible indication of God's will, when they concur with the inward promptings of the Spirit and with the Word of God. So long as they are stationary, wait. When you must act, they will open, and a way will be made through oceans and rivers, wastes and rocks.[10]

There are so many examples of this in the Bible, but one really stands out for me, and I hope it will be meaningful for you as well. It is the story of Joseph—a story of moving from powerlessness to power.

When the Joseph of the Old Testament was seventeen, he had a couple of dreams in which his ten older brothers bowed down to him. We know this was God's Spirit speaking prophetically to Joseph through the dream, but it's not clear from Scripture whether he was completely aware of it at the time. He then made the mistake, or so it seems, of sharing the dreams with his brothers, who didn't take too kindly to what they considered a nightmare. I mean, who jumps up and down with excitement over the opportunity to pay homage to your younger punk brother, who is also Dad's favorite? When the opportunity presented itself to get rid of him, the brothers sold Joseph to a band of gypsies who were on their way to Egypt and told their father that he had been devoured by a ferocious animal. Once in Egypt, Joseph was sold as a slave to Pharaoh's captain of the guard, a guy named Potiphar.

From a human perspective, Joseph's circumstances were horrible and traumatic. And yet, right in the midst of them, the biblical writer noted, "The LORD was with

Joseph so that he prospered" (Genesis 39:2). It is a way of saying that God's Spirit had come to rest on him, much as the Spirit came to rest on Jesus at his baptism. With God's favor, Joseph quickly earned Potiphar's recognition and was appointed head of the household. Joseph's circumstances definitely began to improve, which suggested the possibility that something bigger was going on here.

However, it wasn't long until Joseph experienced a dramatic series of ups and downs, one of which landed him in prison—for years. Even so, we are repeatedly reminded that "the LORD was with him" (v. 21). One of the gifts the Spirit gave to Joseph was the ability to interpret dreams. When Pharaoh, who had been having a recurring bad dream, heard of Joseph's skill set, he retrieved him from prison and asked Joseph to tell him what the dream meant. Joseph replied, "I cannot do it . . . but God will give Pharaoh the answer he desires" (41:16). If he didn't know it before, this statement is evidence that at this point Joseph knew that the Lord was with him.

Through the Spirit's power, Joseph told Pharaoh the meaning of the dream: there would be seven years of a bumper crop, followed by seven years of famine. Joseph then recommended a plan of action to prepare for the famine. Pharaoh made Joseph second in command over all Egypt to oversee the project. Joseph accepted the job.

Two years into the seven years of famine, Jacob (Joseph's father, who still believed Joseph was dead) sent his sons (Joseph's brothers) to Egypt to barter for food.

When they arrived, out of respect for this great leader in Egypt, they bowed down before him. Of course, they had no clue that this was the younger brother they had thrown under the bus so many years before. Joseph was thirty when Pharaoh made him overseer of famine relief, so he was now thirty-nine. It had taken twenty-two years, but the prophetic dreams of a seventeen-year-old boy had finally come true.

After additional encounters, Joseph finally revealed his true identity to his betrayers. With all the power Joseph now had at his disposal, his brothers were terrified about what he was going to do. What would you do? As one who has been betrayed and lived in a prison of despair, I have several ideas in mind, and all of them fall into the category of revenge.

But Joseph had no interest in revenge. Instead, he forgave them! *What?* How did he pull this off? How did he find it in his heart to absolve them of their evil deeds that had ruined his life, or at least had felt like that at many times over the last twenty-two years? Listen in on the private conversation in which Joseph revealed his answer to his brothers:

> Joseph said to his brothers, "I am Joseph! Is my father still living?" But his brothers were not able to answer him, because they were terrified at his presence.
>
> Then Joseph said to his brothers, "Come close to me." When they had done so, he said, "I am your

brother Joseph, the one you sold into Egypt! And now, do not be distressed and do not be angry with yourselves for selling me here, because it was to save lives that God sent me ahead of you. For two years now there has been famine in the land, and for the next five years there will be no plowing and reaping. But God sent me ahead of you to preserve for you a remnant on earth and to save your lives by a great deliverance.

"So then, it was not you who sent me here, but God. He made me father to Pharaoh, lord of his entire household and ruler of all Egypt." (Genesis 45:3–8)

Somewhere in the lower story of his difficult circumstances, Joseph glimpsed the upper story of God's purpose. Instead of pointless suffering, he saw an undeniable set of divine circumstances unfolding that not only confirmed God had a bigger plan, but that Joseph had a leading role to play in its unfolding. It was God's will for Joseph to be in Egypt in time to save not just the people of Egypt but also the people of Israel. In that greater plan, his brothers weren't the villains so much as secondary characters with a cameo appearance. Once Joseph put this all together and saw the redemptive purpose in his circumstances, it enabled him to forgive his brothers of their betrayal.

What is true for Joseph is also true for us. God often communicates his will through our circumstances. It will likely take some time to discern it, but keep your eyes open and in time you will see it and have the confidence to move forward as Joseph did. God uses multiple means to speak his will to us. When there is alignment, there will also be increased confidence.

F. B. Meyer penned these insightful words:

> God's impressions within and His Word without are always corroborated by His Providence around, and we should quietly wait until those three focus into one point. . . .
>
> If you do not know what you ought to do, stand still until you do. And when the time comes for action, circumstances, like glow-worms, will sparkle along your path; and you will become so sure that you are right, when God's three witnesses concur, that you could not be surer though an angel beckoned you on.
>
> The circumstances of our daily life are to us an infallible indication of God's will, when they concur with the inward promptings of the Spirit and with the Word of God.[11]

I don't know about you, but I have definitely had a few times over the years when my circumstances sparkled like glowworms, including some recent experiences that are part of the story I've been sharing.

What about you? Seen any glowworms recently? If not, here's a suggestion. Take some time to identify seasons in the past when you feel God did speak through your circumstances. Whether it was at the time or years later, what helped you recognize the upper story of God's bigger plan in the lower story of your circumstances? Then consider whether or not there might be any parallels between your past experiences and your current circumstances. If you could give your circumstances a voice, what might they say to you? If you find it helpful, write out your memories and observations. You may even want to share what you write with a friend or mentor, who might see the glowworms you miss.

The one word of caution about listening for God's voice in circumstances is that not every circumstance contains a message from God. Dallas Willard said it best:

> The mere open or closed doors of circumstances cannot function independently of the other two lights . . . for one does not know merely by looking at these doors who is opening or closing them—God, Satan, or another human being. Indeed, one often cannot tell whether they are open or closed until after one has acted. It is not, therefore, practically possible to use the criteria of openness or closedness by themselves to determine what to do. Scripture and inner promptings must be brought into consideration to determine whether doors are open or closed.[12]

Exercise caution when listening to your circumstances, and keep your focus on where God's Word, the voice of the Spirit, and your circumstances "focus into one point," as F. B. Meyer put it. Resist the temptation to force fit an alignment in your mind that gets you what you want but isn't necessarily what God has in mind. So, be careful, for sure, but don't let this caution keep you from recognizing that God is very much alive and active in your world. He is close to you and is at work in the circumstances of your life. Just as he was with Joseph, the Lord is with you. Look closely and you will see it.

TIME TO ALIGN

Up until my experience of betrayal, I felt I had a proven track record of experiencing God guiding me through his Word, through the still, small voice of the Spirit, and through his undeniable involvement in the circumstances of my life. It led me to some pretty awesome places, which is why I felt I was at an 8 on the empowerment scale. But then the betrayal hit, and out of nowhere I was in a deep hole and struggling to find my way out. It was humiliating and embarrassing to free-fall from an 8 to a 2.

My journey to recovery began, as I mentioned in chapter 2, when I allowed myself to become vulnerable in my powerlessness. I had to empty myself of control in the areas I could not control and turn everything over to God. I silently whispered and sometimes even shouted this prayer over and over again: *My life has become unmanageable. God, I need your help.* Eventually, it started to take.

Then it was time for phase two. Just as Jesus did, I needed to surrender my will and align my life completely with the will of God. I knew this was how I needed to live.

Aligned with the Word

My next step was clear. I didn't need to pray about it any more than Jesus needed to pray about the three responses he gave to Satan in the wilderness. I must forgive those who betrayed me. How could I be okay with God forgiving my sins and then refuse to forgive those who had sinned against me? I'd seen too many people get caught in the quicksand of bitterness. You have probably heard the adage "They are hurting no one but themselves." Not forgiving someone is like ingesting poison and expecting the other person to die. I knew I didn't want to live or die that way.

I remember the first time I gave this a try. I not only offered forgiveness to my betrayers, but also asked them to forgive me of anything I had done against them. To be honest, at this point I didn't fully know all they actually had done against me. The conversation went well, like a good Christian movie. All the right things were said, and I think we even ended with a prayer. It was the right thing to do, but frankly, it didn't take. Another old adage rang true for me—I forgave but I couldn't forget. I tried, but I could not stop reliving all the painful memories.

Over time, as more information came out about what had actually happened, I knew I needed to let it go, but it was hard. I made it my practice, out of obedience to

God, to forgive them over and over again in my prayers. Sometimes, I actually felt nauseous as I prayed. I was trying to live in obedience, but I wasn't experiencing any of the relief I desperately needed. I was relying on a principle I had taught for years—blessing follows obedience, not the other way around—but the blessing part continued to elude me. In the end, the full relief I sought wouldn't come for two more years.

I don't think my struggle to forgive is all that unique. In fact, I think it may be one of the most common struggles human beings encounter. You have some sort of pain, some sort of trauma or struggle, and you just can't shake it or leave it behind. It might be caused by any number of things.

- You got passed over for a promotion.
- You made a mistake.
- You lost all your money and had to start over.
- You found out you have a chronic disease or a life-threatening illness.
- You turned a certain age and concluded that life had passed you by.
- You were sued.
- You experienced a series of setbacks over time and eventually gave up trying.
- You were in a terrible car accident.
- You lost someone you deeply loved and relied on.
- You were accused of something you didn't do.
- You _____.

Whatever that thing is or was for you, you have to find some way to leave it behind. To leave something behind doesn't mean living in denial or pretending whatever happened doesn't really matter. If you lost someone, that person isn't coming back.... That's hard. If you have a chronic disease, it isn't going away.... That's hard. If you have to start over from financial ruin, your circumstance will be tenuous.... That's hard.

From a prison cell, here is what Paul wrote after declaring that he wanted to know Christ and the power of his resurrection:

> Not that I have already obtained all this, or have already arrived at my goal, but I press on to take hold of that for which Christ Jesus took hold of me. Brothers and sisters, I do not consider myself yet to have taken hold of it. But one thing I do: *Forgetting what is behind and straining toward what is ahead*, I press on toward the goal to win the prize for which God has called me heavenward in Christ Jesus. (Philippians 3:12–14, emphasis added)

To move forward as Paul did, you have to forget or set aside what is behind, no matter how hard it is to do or how long it takes. Your dreams for the future must grow bigger than the painful memories of the past.

Whether your powerlessness is the result of something that happened to you or the result of personal struggles, it has no doubt beaten you down. Chances are good that to move forward into God's calling, there is something you need to leave behind. It may involve forgiving someone or even forgiving yourself. Or it may involve entrusting God with questions for which there may be no answers this side of eternity.

God's Word is clear—the past belongs in the past. Because he is a good Father and wants the best for us, we can trust his word to us. Don't gloss over what you have to leave behind too quickly. Believe me: I know how easy it is to do just that. You will likely not be able to let go of whatever you need to leave behind in one sitting (I certainly wasn't), but every small step you take away from the past gets you that much closer to the better future that lies ahead of you.

Aligned with the Spirit

The Word was clear about my need to forgive, but it also gave me great freedom and latitude in terms of pursuing my future. From a scriptural point of view, I felt I had many options as long as my heart was fully aligned with God. As I turned my attention to discerning my next step vocationally, this is where I began to lean into the still, small voice of the Spirit for direction and guidance.

From the time I was fifteen years old, my calling had been to be a pastor. From the age of fifteen to fifty-five (yes, forty whole years), God sustained my life as I kept my hand imperfectly to the plow. Overall (meaning there were many ups and downs), every season of ministry had been extremely positive, and God's vision for me far exceeded anything and everything I had ever dreamed of.

Then the still, small voice came. *Cities*, it whispered. It wasn't spoken to my ears but to my spirit—from Spirit to spirit. I sensed God wanted me to do something new and extraordinary—to no longer focus on growing a single congregation but to focus instead on uniting multiple churches within a city. I began to have a vision for the kind of unity Jesus prayed for: "that they may be one" (John 17:11). Although I didn't yet know exactly what that meant, I believed I was being called to play a role in it.

When it became clear that the elders of the church I was serving did not feel called to lead this movement, I stepped down with their blessing. I then approached three men, all older and wiser than me, to serve on my "personal board of directors." These men supported me financially and also committed to help me navigate the next steps of my calling.

But then it was just a few months later that I discovered the betrayal, and my chronic deep depression set in. At this point I thought I was done. I have already shared that part of my story with you, so now it's time to tell you what happened next.

This is where my circumstances began to line up with the Word of God and the still, small voice.

Aligned with Circumstances

A church in Kansas City came on my radar. They were looking for a lead teaching pastor. To be honest, I had little interest in the opportunity. Been there, done that—three times. Rozanne and I had an amazing community established in our neighborhood north of San Antonio. Plus, our grandkids were just a few minutes down the road. We also weren't thrilled about changing climates. There can be terrible tornadoes in Kansas— just ask Dorothy—not to mention the fact that it snows there. I had done the snow thing twice already, and I wasn't keen on signing up for round three of frigid winters.

But as we probed just a little, we discovered that this church had a history and a heart to humbly run point on bringing churches together for kingdom impact. The still, small voice whispered the word *cities* to me again. Even so, I was determined to shake it off. I won't bore you with the hundred ways I did this, but believe me, I did.

Then, in the course of one week, all three members of my personal board of directors communicated they felt this was the direction I should take. I hadn't seen that coming. When I pushed back and said, "But I don't want to move to Kansas," they essentially said, "What does that have to do with anything? This opportunity has everything to do with aligning your life with the will of God as best we understand it. This role perfectly fits the new call on your life, which we agree with and support, and it draws on your strongest gift set. Your circumstances have absolutely closed in San Antonio, but God's timing and hand are all pointing to Kansas City." Although they felt certain, I remained in cringe mode. I thought that my fears about aligning my will with the will of God were now being realized—this was not all fun and games, and I did not like where things were going.

Then my daughter and son-in-law asked to meet with Rozanne and me. "We want to move to Kansas City with you guys!" That was the first thing they said. *What! Come again?* Then they proceeded to share their hearts with us. Our son-in-law had been raised not too far from Kansas City, and both he and my daughter loved the Midwest and the four seasons. They also loved baseball, and Kansas City is a big sports town. They wanted to go on this adventure with us. The harder I tried to push the opportunity away, the more my circumstances seemed to be lining up to match the sense of calling we felt in our spirits from the Spirit.

We finally said yes to candidacy and allowed the process to move forward. The congregation in Kansas City showered us with a unanimous vote of affirmation. Even after this, I delayed accepting their invitation for almost two months. I wanted to be sure this was as close as I could get to God's will for our lives. I didn't want this to be about me but about God's kingdom.

It was at this time that my depression began to lift. I am not saying I bounced back completely to my old self.

Frankly, I didn't want to go back to my old self. I wanted a deeper, stronger me to emerge out of the ashes. My soul was still bruised and tender, but I had definitely turned a corner. I was eating again, sleeping again, laughing again, even singing again. I also found myself thinking more about the future than the past. The transformation for which I had hoped and prayed was finally taking place right before my eyes.

YOUR TURN

I hope you are already thinking about what aligning your life to God's will might look like for you. It doesn't need to involve a move to Kansas City, though we would love to have you here. It could be something super big, something super hard, or maybe just a few small changes. It may be striking out in a completely new direction or simply finding greater contentment and purpose in what you are already doing. Whatever aligning your life with God's will might require, the most important thing is the attitude of your heart. Open your hands to heaven and pray for the will of the Father in heaven to fall down on you. Then ask for the power and the courage you need to live it out.

I can imagine you might be thinking something like, "Hey! It's a bit scary to surrender that kind of control when I don't know where it might lead." Tell me about it!

Jumping into the spiritual equivalent of a wheelbarrow that is going to be pushed across a massive waterfall on a tiny tightrope *is* scary. But remember what's on the other side—your future filled with power. And the One who is carrying you forward is God.

So, what is that scary thing God is inviting you to move toward? The possibilities are endless. God might be asking you to:

- forgive someone who has deeply hurt you
- break off a toxic relationship
- start taking care of yourself
- go back to school
- start something new
- join a small group, a support group, or a recovery group
- get help for an addiction or any self-defeating habit
- retire from your job and devote your time to helping people

If what God is asking you to do is clearly written in his Word, you don't need to pray about it. Just do it in faith. If God's Word is not clear, then there is more liberty and possibly multiple acceptable options and approaches. Once your hands are open to God's will, find ways to listen for the still, small voice—the whisper of the Spirit speaking directly to your spirit. Consider your circumstances, looking for open doors to walk through and shut doors to walk away from. Occasionally, God's Spirit also invites us to bust through seemingly closed doors, especially if we are trapped in situations such as addiction or abuse.

Surround yourself with a spiritual community of folks who get you, believe in you, and can help you navigate your direction. Invite them to help you pay attention to your circumstances, especially circumstances that reinforce the truths of God's Word and echo the whispers of the still, small voice.

If you're afraid you might mess up, I feel you on this. But here is what I have come to understand. If your heart is genuinely open before God, he promises to be your guide: "If any of you lacks wisdom, you should ask God, who gives generously to all without finding fault, and it will be given to you" (James 1:5).

Charles Blondin did end up getting a volunteer, someone who said yes. It was a man named Harry Colcord. Instead of climbing into a wheelbarrow, he jumped on Blondin's back. Here are the instructions Blondin gave him: "Look up, Harry . . . you are no longer Colcord, you are Blondin. Until I clear this place be a part of me, mind, body, and soul. If I sway, sway with me. Do not attempt to do any balancing yourself."[13]

They successfully crossed to the other side.

Jesus extends a similar invitation to us. During our journey here on earth, we must become one with Jesus—mind, body, and soul. That's how we will make it over to the other side—to that place where we can access his mighty strength, the same power that raised Jesus from the dead.

Any volunteers?

PART III

Empowered

CHAPTER 5

How Jesus Rose
from the Dead

When I was a little boy, I dreamed of being a super-hero. Any superhero would do, but my favorite was Ultraman. Ultraman was the star of the coolest show aired on television between 1966 and 1967. I was just five years old at the time.

Here's Ultraman's backstory. When a monster space alien named Bemular traveled to Earth in an orb of blue energy, he was followed in hot pursuit by none other than Ultraman, who traveled in an orb of red energy. Meanwhile on earth, Science Patrol Officer Shin Hayata was sent in a small submarine to investigate the landing of a mysterious blue orb in a nearby lake. As fate would have it, Ultraman in his red orb inadvertently collided with Shin Hayata's sub, and Hayata was killed. Feeling guilty for killing Hayata, Ultraman revived him in exchange for Hayata becoming Ultraman's host while he remained on earth to defend humans against aliens and monsters such as Bemular. How cool is that?

Ultraman was a tall character in a stainless-steel suit of armor. He had an oval head, two oversized bug eyes, and a light called a Color Timer, which was connected to his heart and visible at the center of his chest. His superhero powers and his life force came from solar energy, which was heavily reduced by Earth's filtering atmosphere. As a result, he could only remain on earth for three minutes at a time, and the Color Timer was an indicator of his health and energy level. At full health, the Color Timer was a greenish-blue color. However, as the minutes ticked by, the light turned red, indicating that his power was running out. When it started to blink, Ultraman was in the danger zone. If Ultraman ran out of time or energy, the light would turn black and he would die. As you might suspect, every episode had Ultraman on the brink of death, causing little boys like me to hold our breath and scoot closer to the television. In the end, Ultraman always won. That is what superheroes do.

For Halloween in 1966 my parents purchased an Ultraman costume for me at the local Kmart. When I put on the outfit, I became Ultraman. This suit of steel (actually polyester) not only helped me to bag some amazing candy that October 31, but also helped me for several days after as I saved the world from space monsters a million times over and even rescued many damsels in distress. Why has a space monster never come after you? Because I took him out before he got to you. You're welcome.

The imaginary worlds we live in as children are great. We still believe anything is possible. But when we become adults, it's time to take off our superhero capes and get on with real life. And yet, there are ways that childhood ability to believe amazing things can still serve us well even now. In fact, you may want to sit down for this because I'm about to make a crazy connection between Ultraman and us.

Here it is: faith in Christ gives us access to superhero-level power. No, I am not kidding. Feast your eyes on Paul's statement to the believers in Ephesus:

> I pray that the eyes of your heart may be enlightened in order that you may know the hope to which he has called you, the riches of his glorious inheritance in his holy people, and his *incomparably great power for us who believe. That power is the same as the mighty strength he exerted when he raised Christ from the dead* and seated him at his right hand in the heavenly realms. (Ephesians 1:18–20, emphasis added)

Paul told us that "the same power that raised Jesus from the dead also lives in us." That's more power than even Ultraman possessed. So maybe we need to hold off on putting away those capes and dig in a little deeper to discover how we might tap into this power.

The secret? There is no secret! Everything we need to know is found in the life of Jesus. As we discovered in chapter 1, Jesus placed himself in an extremely vulnerable position; he became human and embraced all the limitations that come with it. But Jesus still had access to a power that enabled him to perform miracles, heal people, and even rise from the dead. If he left all his divine power behind in the heavens, where did his miracle-working power come from? The answer to this question is found in Jesus' baptism.

THE SOURCE OF JESUS' POWER

We don't know much about Jesus from birth to age thirty except that he continued to grow in wisdom and stature (Luke 2:52). But Jesus was undeniably on the scene the day he was baptized by John. I missed this clue about the source of Jesus' power for many years, but now I see it so plainly.

Here is how the story went down. John the Baptist, who was baptizing at the Jordan River, saw Jesus walking toward him and declared, "Look, the Lamb of God, who takes away the sin of the world!" (John 1:29). John's Jewish listeners knew exactly what that phrase "Lamb of God" meant. Throughout Israelite history perfect lambs were sacrificed to atone for the sins of God's people. The lambs were both literal and symbolic, pointing to the messianic Lamb of God who would one day be sacrificed for the sins of the entire world—past, present, and future (Hebrews 10:1–10).

John then proclaimed, "This is the one I meant when I said, 'A man who comes after me has surpassed me because he was before me'" (John 1:30). John wasn't saying Jesus was born before him, because he wasn't. John was born first. He was acknowledging that Jesus was not merely a human, but God in the flesh—fully God, fully human. Jesus was with God in the beginning because he is God (v. 2).

When John baptized Jesus, something dramatic happened—something that hadn't happened to anyone else John had baptized.

> As soon as Jesus was baptized, he went up out of the water. At that moment heaven was opened, and he saw the Spirit of God descending like a dove and alighting on him. And a voice from heaven said, "This is my Son, whom I love; with him I am well pleased."
> (Matthew 3:16–17)

God the Father, the first person of the Trinity, declared his association with and his approval of Jesus, and the mission Jesus formally began that day.

Did you catch the clue that answers the question about where Jesus got his power to do miracles? It happened when the Holy Spirit descended on Jesus like a dove. The Holy Spirit is the third person of the Trinity. The Spirit is fully God, endowed with all the traits of God—omniscience, omnipotence, and omnipresence.

Why might God part the heavens and make a dramatic public statement about Jesus in this way? It is certainly a ceremonial anointing and commissioning for ministry

(Acts 10:38), but there is more. The Spirit wasn't making a cameo appearance at the Jordan, walking across the stage of Jesus' life only to exit again on the other side. In the apostle John's account of Jesus' baptism, he recorded what John the Baptist said about recognizing Jesus as the Messiah:

> And I myself did not know him, but the one who sent me to baptize with water told me, "The man on whom you see the Spirit come down and remain is the one who will baptize with the Holy Spirit." (John 1:33)

The Spirit didn't do a fly-by. The Spirit came down and *remained* with Jesus.

Jesus would later describe the Holy Spirit using a word the New Testament writers captured with the Greek word *parakletos* (often referred to by scholars today as the "Paraclete"):

> I will ask the Father, and he will give you another advocate [*parakletos*] to help you and be with you forever—the Spirit of truth. (14:16–17)

> The Advocate [*parakletos*], the Holy Spirit, whom the Father will send in my name, will teach you all things and will remind you of everything I have said to you. (v. 26)

Parakletos is a cognate or derivative of the verb *parakaleo*. It is a compound word, meaning it includes two words—*para* and *kaleo*. *Para* means "near, beside, or alongside." *Kaleo* means "to call."[1] Together, the two words form *parakletos* and refer to one who is called to come alongside, a helper, an advocate.

Coming alongside is exactly what the Holy Spirit did as Jesus was baptized and officially began his ministry. The Spirit publicly commissioned Jesus for the work he would do over the next three years, but the Spirit also remained with Jesus and empowered him for the duration of his ministry.

What, specifically, did the Spirit empower Jesus to do? The apostle Paul later summarized it this way:

> You know what has happened throughout the province of Judea, beginning in Galilee after the baptism that John preached—how God anointed Jesus of Nazareth *with the Holy Spirit and power*, and how he went around doing good and healing all who were under the power of the devil, because God was with him. (Acts 10:37–38, emphasis added)

The Holy Spirit came alongside Jesus to be his power source. Where would Jesus find the power to do the will of the Father? In the person of the Holy Spirit, who remained with him. We see this clearly in the very next verse that follows Matthew's description of Jesus' baptism:

> Then Jesus was led by the Spirit into the wilderness to
> be tempted by the devil. (Matthew 4:1)

The Holy Spirit didn't return to the heavens after the baptism, nor did the Spirit come and go on an as-needed basis. The Holy Spirit *remained* with Jesus to guide him and empower him—day by day, hour by hour, moment by moment. Jesus didn't lead himself into the wilderness; the Spirit did. Why? To complete an essential component in God's master plan of salvation. As we discussed in chapter 1, the apostle Paul referred to that master plan when he described Jesus as the second Adam (1 Corinthians 15:45–47).

Jesus, the second Adam, was led into the wilderness where he would be tempted, just as the first Adam was tempted (Hebrews 4:15). Unlike the first Adam, Jesus triumphed over the Tempter. What did his victory accomplish? The writer of Hebrews told us:

> For this reason he had to be made like them, fully
> human in every way, in order that he might become a
> merciful and faithful high priest in service to God, and
> that he might make atonement for the sins of the people.
> Because he himself suffered when he was tempted, he
> is able to help those who are being tempted. (2:17–18)

Jesus did not sin. That means when he was offered up on the cross as atonement or payment for sin, his sacrifice was sufficient. When we accept God's offer of salvation, we die to our association with the first Adam and are "born again," this time into the family of Jesus, the second Adam (John 3:3–8). This is the gospel, the good news. This was the will of God for his Son, and it is precisely why the Spirit led Jesus into the wilderness that day.

Up to this point, Jesus hadn't done any miracles.[2] He hadn't healed anyone or raised anyone from the dead. But now that the Spirit had come alongside him, the floodgates of power were released and the miracles would follow. From that point on, whenever Jesus received his Father's divine clearance, he healed, provided, and even raised the dead—all by the power of the Holy Spirit.

As we saw in chapter 1, Jesus confirmed his power source when he healed a demon-possessed man born blind and mute, restoring his sight and speech (Matthew 12:22–28). The religious leaders then suggested that Jesus' power came from Satan, the prince of demons (v. 24). As part of his rebuttal, Jesus said:

> "But if it is by the Spirit of God that I drive out demons, then the kingdom of God has come upon you." (v. 28)

Throughout all my years of theological study and decades in ministry, I never zeroed in on the foundational truth about divine power that Jesus revealed here. I just assumed that Jesus, as God, cast out demons from the well-spring of his own power. But he didn't. He relied on the Holy Spirit to channel power through him to accomplish this miracle, as well as all the miracles recorded in the Gospels.

There are thirty-five miracles contained in the four gospel accounts of the life of Jesus. Twenty-three are healings, nine demonstrate Jesus' power over nature, and three involve raising people from the dead.[3] What do all thirty-five miracles have in common? Each one was in the center of the Father's will, and each one was powered by the Holy Spirit through Jesus.

The biggest miracle of all is the resurrection of Jesus from the dead. How did Jesus pull off this supreme miracle? He didn't! It was the power of the Spirit that raised Jesus from the dead, the same Spirit that had remained with him throughout his thirty-three-year journey on earth. The Scriptures repeatedly affirm this:

> That power is the same as the mighty strength he [God] exerted when he raised Christ from the dead and seated him at his right hand in the heavenly realms. (Ephesians 1:19–20)

> In his earthly life [Jesus] was born into King David's family line, and he was shown to be the Son of God when he was raised from the dead by the power of

the Holy Spirit. He is Jesus Christ our Lord. (Romans 1:3–4 NLT)

And if the Spirit of him who raised Jesus from the dead is living in you, he who raised Christ from the dead will also give life to your mortal bodies because of his Spirit who lives in you. (Romans 8:11)

For Christ also suffered once for sins, the righteous for the unrighteous, to bring you to God. He was put to death in the body but made alive in the Spirit. (1 Peter 3:18)

Paul continued to drive home the Spirit's role in empowering the life and ministry of Jesus in his first letter to Timothy:

Beyond all question, the mystery from which true godliness springs is great:

> He appeared in the flesh,
>> was vindicated by the Spirit,
> was seen by angels,
>> was preached among the nations,
> was believed on in the world,
>> was taken up in glory.
>>> (1 Timothy 3:16)

The mystery Paul spoke about here is the source that produces godliness in God's people. That source is revealed through the life of Jesus. His appearance in the flesh refers to his life in human form. His vindication by the Spirit refers to his resurrection from the dead, which was witnessed by angels (Matthew 28:2). When Jesus rose from the dead, it proved that he was the Son of God and reversed the death sentence that humanity inherited from the first Adam, giving us the opportunity for vindication. Christ's victory over death ignited a worldwide movement to preach Christ to the nations. Paul finished with Christ's ascension to the Father, where he reclaimed his place at God's right hand. The Spirit was the power source from which Jesus drove out demons, performed miracles, and even rose from the dead.

If you'll allow me to go a little rogue again to make a point, there are some similarities between Jesus and Shin Hayata. Jesus subjected himself to a life of human limitations. Shin Hayata, Ultraman's human host, had no powers of his own. At Jesus' baptism, the Holy Spirit took up residence within the body of Jesus. After he was revived, Shin Hayata became Ultraman's physical host on earth. Jesus drew upon the power of the Holy Spirit, a real person, for every miraculous thing he did throughout his three years of ministry. Shin Hayata channeled Ultraman's superpowers to fight evil on earth. But here's where the analogy breaks down. While we don't have access to Ultraman's power source, we do have access to Jesus' power source.

Is this sinking in yet? Read the previous paragraph again if your heart rate didn't spike. Jesus' supernatural power is available to you and to me. It is how we can rise above our powerlessness and tap into a source of unlimited strength. If you don't want to access this kind of power, check your pulse and make sure your heart is beating. As for me, I am ready to dive in with both feet.

OUR EMPOWERMENT

For most of my Christian life, I assumed Jesus just had an advantage. He was God and therefore had the power to do whatever he wanted or needed. Now, I realize that this was not the case. Jesus emptied himself of these amazing powers because he didn't want to have the advantage. He voluntarily put himself in a place of extreme vulnerability so he would have to rely on the Father's will to guide his steps and on the Holy Spirit for the power he needed to pull it all off.

Jesus was limited, just like you and me, and yet he performed amazing miracles. Not only that, he also taught that we have access to that same power and more:

> Very truly I tell you, whoever believes in me will do the works I have been doing, and they will do even greater things than these, because I am going to the Father. (John 14:12)

And on another occasion, he said:

If you have faith as small as a mustard seed, you can say to this mulberry tree, "Be uprooted and planted in the sea," and it will obey you. (Luke 17:6)

This is almost too unbelievable to take in, at least for me. Yet, the Scriptures clearly affirm that it is so.

While I found it fascinating to think I could access the power Jesus used to perform miracles, all I wanted while in the midst of my depression was to return to a state of mental health. How could I hope to have the power to move a mountain when I couldn't even find enough peace in my soul to experience just a normal day?

I wanted to find out how I could tap into the power at the entry level, the kind of power that would help me become whole again. Then I would be happy to move on into those "greater things" Jesus talked about. But when I was in the depths of my journey through powerlessness, I doubted that I could learn to access this power for my own healing. Even so, I wanted it. It was my hope.

How about you? If you placed yourself on the low end of the empowerment scale, then perhaps you can relate to how I felt. Maybe you think these promises might be true for a select group of people—apostles, prophets, pastors, missionaries, priests, nuns—but not for you. If so, I understand. I'm a pastor and I still felt this way. More than once I even wondered if I should give up being a pastor altogether.

My encouragement to you is to allow these promises to be true not just generally, but specifically—for you. Let your heart believe. Lean in. This is the Word of God we are talking about here. The promise of access to power comes from Jesus himself. This doesn't mean there is a spiritual switch you can flip and, presto, you're no longer powerless. At least, that's not my story. But I didn't want to just give up and live in a pit of hopelessness forever. I couldn't. I wanted more. I want the same for you.

So maybe it's time to strap on a cape and claim our rightful place in the world of superheroes—because that is who we are in Christ. We have a source of supernatural power residing right inside of us. Our Color Timer might be blinking red right now, but the power source is there.

What does it mean to put on a superhero cape? It means we lay claim to our power. I'm going to share some insights about how to do that, but first I need to give you a heads-up. Some of what you read may strike you as the kind of "rah-rah" talk I promised early on I would not dish out. "Rah-rah" speech is defined as uncritical enthusiasm.[4] It is optimism without cause. I have little patience for this kind of rhetoric. What I present below about our power is optimism and enthusiasm based on truth. There is a huge difference between that and rah-rah talk.

Here's why this matters. We know from scientific research that the human brain is actually capable of changing and restructuring itself.[5] Scientists refer to this as "neuroplasticity." The apostle Paul called it the "renewing of your mind" (Romans 12:2). Repetition is one factor that has been demonstrated to shape the mind. Whatever you hear over and over again, you start to believe. If someone repeatedly says you're ugly and worthless, you will likely start to believe it. If someone repeatedly tells you that you are beautiful and valuable beyond measure, you will likely believe that instead—particularly if the one speaking is God himself. So, as you continue your journey toward greater empowerment, it's important to reset your mind on what the Bible says is absolutely true about you. Nothing rah-rah about that!

So, how do we lay claim to our power? We immerse ourselves in truth. Romans 8 identifies many of the empowering truths we can claim because the Holy Spirit, our divine power source, resides within us. Each one is phrased as a claim you can make, right now, to reset your mind on truth.

I claim that no one can condemn me (Romans 8:1). Why? Because "the law of the Spirit who gives life has set you free from the law of sin and death" (v. 2). If God does not and will not condemn you, why would you let mere human beings condemn you? With the Spirit of the living God in you, no one has the right to tear you down, declare you will never amount to anything, or dehumanize you.

Now, if you've had your internal power source drained by the kryptonite of human condemnation, claiming this truth once probably won't do the trick—it didn't work that way for me. But there were two things that did help me overcome the condemning messages of my betrayers. First, this claim to power works a little like an antibiotic prescribed to fight off a nasty bacterial infection ravaging your body. One dose isn't enough. You have to complete the whole course—a consistent dosage over a period of time—to kill the infection completely. I had to claim this truth over and over again to fight off the bacteria of betrayal.

The second thing that really helped was when a trusted friend declared this truth over me. I was so beaten down that I didn't believe my own voice. But when someone I trusted claimed it for me, it made it easier for me to believe this truth for myself.

I claim that I will overcome death (Romans 8:11). In Christ, you have been forgiven of your sin. The grave will not be able to hold you any more than it did Jesus. You will rise again. The Spirit in you is a deposit guaranteeing this transaction (Ephesians 1:14).

In the midst of my depression, the only thing I wanted was to start living again. And yet, this truth about overcoming death really did help me. It gave me the long-term view, which promised a good ending. Even if I never licked my powerlessness in this life, the Holy Spirit would step in to ensure that I won in the end. It relieved some of the pressure I felt to pull myself up by my bootstraps and "get over it." Instead, I could remind myself, "God's got you. Relax, Randy. Breathe."

I claim that I am a child of God (Romans 8:14). You

are a child of God, but it doesn't stop there. As an heir to all that belongs to God, you will be a coheir with Jesus in the kingdom to come. It may be hard for you to say it out loud, but it is completely true: you are a somebody! Don't deny it any longer. Walk humbly in the confidence that you are a child of God.

This claim is about your new identity. This may be a particularly powerful claim for you if you have ever been marginalized, abandoned, beaten down, or stripped of human dignity. In the midst of my depression, I found it helpful to say the following prayer every morning before anyone other than God had access to me: "God, today someone may try to rob me of the identity and dignity that are mine in Jesus. Before they have a chance to make their move, I declare that my identity and my dignity are not up for grabs—not today, not tomorrow, not ever."

Some days, the bullies may still get the best of you, but if you continue to make this declaration over and over again, it will begin to sink into your soul.

I claim that I am no longer a slave to fear (Romans 8:15). If fear has left you powerless, it's time to say, "No more!" The power of the One within you is immensely more powerful than anything you can fear. The more "cape time" you log—living in the power of the Spirit— the less likely you are to give in to fear.

Even though I am now on the other side of my season of intense struggle, anxiety is still an issue for me. Anxiety differs from fear. While fear is a temporary response to an actual threat, anxiety is a sustained response to an anticipated threat. In this season of my life, I am fortunate to have very little cause for fear. I know this isn't true for many people, and it will not always be true of my life, but right now, I'm not facing any actual threats of consequence. I struggle more with anxiety.

Anxiety happens when we encounter or imagine a threat and can't move on. I have become quite gifted at imagining threats. In any situation I face, I can play out a series of potential negative outcomes and then worry about them as if they had happened. Sounds crazy, right? I bet you may have done something like this a time or two yourself.

I am now much more proactive in distinguishing between real threats that have actually happened and imagined threats that haven't. It's okay to have a jolt of adrenaline when a lion jumps out of the woods and stares you down as if you were a piece of bacon. That is a good thing. But getting worked up over imagined threats is not good. For me, making that distinction actually takes care of a large percentage of my anxiety problem.

I love how Holocaust survivor Corrie ten Boom put it: "Worrying doesn't empty tomorrow of its sorrow, it empties today of its strength."[6] Whether the threat we face is real or imagined, God is bigger than them both. It's just true.

I claim that in all things God is working for my good (Romans 8:28). This is not mere wishful thinking; it is a promise from God himself specifically for "those who love him" and have aligned their lives to his purpose. You may not like the story you're living now, but it is not how your story ends. This promise may be hard to embrace when you are in a pit and can see no way out, but reach out and grab hold of it because it is true. Repeat after me: *This is not how my story ends. This is not how my story ends. This is not how my story ends.*

Repeating this phrase really did help me. What has helped me even more is finally getting to the other side of my trouble and discovering it is true. The next time I run up against a season of trial, and I will, I will be way more confident of this truth and won't linger in the pit as long. If you've come through a hard season in the past, you probably already know exactly what I am talking about.

I claim that if God is for me, no one can be against me (Romans 8:31). There are so many people and so many circumstances that are bigger and stronger than us, so it's no surprise that many of us walk this planet feeling intimidated. No more! Why? Because God has declared us right with him, and no one can take that away from us. We already belong to him for eternity—nothing can change that. When you enter a dark season or find yourself struggling in a difficult relationship, enter into it with confidence and a commitment to stand for the truth and your dignity because you belong to God without condition. People who wear the cape know this.

I claim that I am more than a conqueror (Romans 8:37). You may be familiar with the Nike brand of athletic gear. The brand name is derived from Nike, the winged

Greek goddess of victory. The brand's logo is derived from the wing or "swoosh" of the goddess, which "symbolizes the sound of speed, movement, power, and motivation."[7]

When Paul wrote that we are "more than conquerors," he used the Greek word *hypernikao*. This is a compound word, meaning it is two words combined into one. *Hyper* is an intensifier of any word that follows it. As the verb form of *nike* (victory), *nikao* means "to be victorious." When you put the two words together, *hypernikao* means we are not merely victorious, but *overwhelmingly* victorious, or as Paul said, "more than conquerors."

When we face situations that intensify our sense of powerlessness—trouble, calamity, persecution, hunger, or even the threat of death, we can claim with confidence that we are *hypernikao*—we are, even now, overwhelmingly victorious through Christ. We aren't merely projected to win someday in the future; we have already won. We are recipients of the victory Christ won on our behalf when he died on the cross in our place. What a difference it would make if we would strap on this attitude every day.

I claim that nothing can separate me from the love of God (Romans 8:39). Here is the biggest and most powerful promise of all. If you've been hurt or abandoned by someone who promised to love you, you might have concluded that you don't deserve to be loved or that you don't want to risk loving again because the pain is too great. You will never have this experience with God. God loved you and me "while we were still sinners" (5:8). He knows everything about you and loves you anyway.

Some people hold back on taking legitimate risks because they fear if they fail, people will think less of them or even shun them. But if you really believe this promise from God, you can take a risk on something you believe in because, in the end, you really have nothing to lose. With the unconditional security of God's love, you can actually fly pretty high in that cape.

These eight claims are just a drop in the bucket when it comes to the power that's available to us, but I hope they give you a good starting point for strapping on your superhero cape. Putting on the cape means you claim your power and do your courageous best to live it out. Imagine what your life might be like if you stopped believing the lies about you. Imagine what your life might be like if you started believing the truths about you. The Holy Spirit within you can give you the power to throw off the lies and embrace the truths.

The Ultraman of my generation never spoke, but it turns out he wasn't the only Ultraman out there. Forty-seven years later, the television series was revived to tell the tale of some other superheroes. And get this—these new Ultramen talk.

In the new series, a young man named Hikaru Raido becomes the willing host of an Ultraman named Ginga. In the last episode of the season, the two have this exchange:

Ultraman Ginga: I will be departing for space.
Go on more adventures on your planet. And
when you're done, we shall meet again.
Hikaru Raido: All right!
Ultraman Ginga: The future can be changed.
It can be for the better or for the worse.
The ones who will decide that are you all.
Farewell. And thank you.[8]

How awesome is that?

Sadly, the Ultraman TV series is make-believe. It took
me a while to come to terms with that, but I finally have.
Our story, on the other hand, is real. Jesus has returned to
the Father, and he invites us to go on more adventures. He
wants our lives to be full—abundantly full (John 10:10
NKJV). He said we would do even greater things than he
did (14:12). We don't have to settle for lives that are flat
and powerless when God has so much more for us, including a divine power source that is available to all who are
willing to reach out and claim it.

Don't allow that condemning voice in your head to
undermine your worth and your confidence—not today,
not tomorrow, not ever.

Don't allow anxiety about what might happen to keep
you from taking legitimate risks.

Don't allow an illness, an accident, or a setback to
convince you that your best days are behind you.

Don't allow your age to convince you that you are too young to get in the game or too old to stay in the game.

Don't allow someone who has hurt or betrayed you to keep you from pursuing the mission God has for you.

Don't allow small-minded people to demean you by stepping on you to make themselves look taller.

Don't quit when you enter into a difficult and confusing season—this is not how your story ends.

Don't back away from a big assignment you believe to be God's will because you are afraid of what you may lose. You have nothing to lose and everything to gain. Make your move!

Don't be afraid even when death itself comes knocking at your door. . . . A resurrection is coming!

Jesus has left you the Paraclete, a source of unlimited power, to come alongside you and to empower the adventures you will take. With your heart surrendered to the will of the Father, and with the power of the Holy Spirit within you, your life can be different than it is now.

As Ultraman Ginga said to Hikaru Raido, the future can be changed. It can be for the better or for the worse. The choice is yours.

Hikaru Raido said "All right!" to adventure. How about you? Are you willing to strap on your cape, to take the next step?

And don't forget Ultraman Ginga's promise: "When you're done, we shall meet again." Is it just me, or does that sound an awful lot like something Jesus once said?

CHAPTER 6

How We Will Rise

In 1904 President Theodore Roosevelt authorized a project that literally moved mountains. The Panama Canal was created to provide a connection between the Atlantic and Pacific Oceans and is considered an engineering marvel to this day. It took ten years and more than forty thousand laborers to complete. This fifty-one-mile stretch of waterway cut through the Isthmus of Panama, which meant ships traveling between New York and California no longer needed to sail around South America. The canal eliminated eight thousand miles from what had been a twelve-thousand-mile trip.[1]

One of the most challenging aspects of the project was the creation of an artificial valley or channel called the Gaillard Cut, which required excavating through some eight miles of mountains. How did they do it? Dynamite! The workers ignited more than seventeen million pounds of dynamite in three years alone. Then they had to remove more than 3.5 billion cubic feet of earth.

For centuries people had dreamed about having a canal, but many declared it was simply an impossible feat. Then some tried but failed. And yet, eventually, a group of determined people made the Panama Canal a reality. And they did it . . . with a whole lot of dynamite.

Dynamite might be one of the best metaphors we have for the kind of power that is available to us in Christ. Anytime we encounter a mountain that keeps us from moving forward and feels impossible to overcome, we need to remember that we have access to divine dynamite. Jesus tells us that we have access to the same explosive power he had—we *can* overcome our mountains. We do so in a strength that doesn't come from humans but from the Spirit of God.

THE GIFT OF POWER

Look at the last thing Jesus said to the disciples before he ascended back to the Father following his resurrection:

> It is not for you to know the times or dates the Father has set by his own authority. But you will receive power when the Holy Spirit comes on you; and you will be my witnesses in Jerusalem, and in all Judea and Samaria, and to the ends of the earth. (Acts 1:7–8)

The disciples had inquired if this was the time when Jesus would at last restore the kingdom to Israel. Jesus reminded them that the timing was not for them to know. You may recall that earlier in Jesus' ministry he let the disciples know that he had no clue when the kingdom would be established—that only the Father knew such things (Mark 13:32). But as soon as Jesus reached his heavenly destination just a few minutes after his final conversation with the disciples, he, too, learned the exact time of his return. The disciples, and the rest of us humans, would remain limited in our knowledge of such things.

And yet the next word Jesus spoke in Acts 1:8 is "but." If you'll allow me to paraphrase, here's how I understand what Jesus told his disciples: "I can't tell you the future—you will still walk around with your same limitations—*but* . . . you are about to receive something even better, and it will change everything. You are going to receive *power*! How will that happen? The Holy Spirit, who has remained with me since my baptism, is going to come down and remain with you. He will be your power source—the same power source I used to do miracles, and the same power source that raised me from the dead!"

The Greek word used for "power" in Jesus' statement is *dunamis*: "But you will receive *dunamis* when the Holy Spirit comes on you." *Dunamis* is the root from which we get our English word—you guessed it—*dynamite*. It's also the root for other power-packed words, such as "dynamo" and "dynamic." *Merriam-Webster* defines dynamite as "an explosive made of nitroglycerin absorbed into porous material."[2] We might say that the kind of power Jesus promised is an explosive made of the Holy Spirit that we absorb through faith in Jesus.

Here is how Luke described what happened when the *dunamis* Jesus promised descended on his followers:

> When the day of Pentecost came, they were all together in one place. Suddenly a sound like the blowing of a violent wind came from heaven and filled the whole house where they were sitting. They saw what seemed to be tongues of fire that separated and came to rest on each of them. All of them were filled with the Holy Spirit and began to speak in other tongues as the Spirit enabled them. (Acts 2:1–4)

When the Holy Spirit came upon and remained with Jesus, we are told it descended on him like a dove. In Acts the Holy Spirit came upon the disciples in the form of fire, a beautiful image of divine power. Once more the Spirit did not come and go, but came to rest on each of them. He had taken up residence within them and would remain with them, just as the Spirit remained with Jesus during his life on earth.

The evidence that something *dynamic* had occurred can readily be seen in the life of Peter. During Jesus' trial and crucifixion, Peter had denied he even knew Jesus—not once but three times (Luke 22:54–62). Peter was weak, afraid, and confused. He was not ready to risk himself for Jesus in any way. No judgment here; I can picture me doing the exact same thing. But the picture we have of Peter after receiving the Holy Spirit couldn't be more different.

It was the day of Pentecost, an annual Jewish celebration of the harvest that brought an estimated one million visitors into Jerusalem from nations all over the world. Seventeen nations are listed in Acts 2:9–11, representing a host of different languages. This is the context Peter was in when he and the disciples stepped out into the streets of Jerusalem to proclaim the gospel. Immediately the Spirit was at work, giving them the ability to communicate in a miraculous way. When Peter and the other disciples spoke, everyone in the crowd heard what they said in their own language. Dynamite!

When some in the crowd suggested the disciples were merely drunk, Peter raised his voice to address them. He proclaimed that, far from being drunk, he and the disciples were the fulfillment of a prophecy recorded by the prophet Joel hundreds of years earlier. He then quoted the prophet:

> "In the last days, God says,
> I will pour out my Spirit on all people.
> Your sons and daughters will prophesy,
> your young men will see visions,
> your old men will dream dreams." (v. 17)

The "last days" about which Joel spoke had now come. The Holy Spirit was being poured out, and Peter, empowered by the Spirit, boldly proclaimed the story of salvation through Jesus. This is the same guy who, just a few weeks earlier, on the night before Jesus' crucifixion, had denied he even knew Jesus when questioned by a young girl. Now he was shouting out the gospel message to a crowd of people who could easily turn on him and take him out. The only difference between Peter before Jesus' crucifixion and now? The Holy Spirit.

By the end of his message, three thousand people had accepted Jesus and were baptized (v. 41). This was the first of many Spirit-empowered things Peter went on to do, including healing people and even raising someone from the dead. Dynamite!

At Pentecost, the power that raised Jesus from the dead was formally and dramatically passed to his followers. And that same power is given to us when we give our lives to Christ. Under our own power, we might be able to overcome some smaller mounds of dirt, but now we have the power within us through the Holy Spirit to take out mountains. Now we just need to learn more about this source of power and how the Spirit deploys his power in and through us.

THE HOLY SPIRIT'S SUPERPOWERS

Every superhero has a superpower. If we think of the Holy Spirit as the ultimate superhero, it can only mean one thing—the Holy Spirit has the ultimate superpowers. So what kind of powers does the Holy Spirit possess, and how does the Holy Spirit deploy those powers in and through us? More specifically, how does the Holy Spirit empower us to overcome the mountains in our lives? The answer: unlimited power!

Remember, the Holy Spirit is fully God, so he has all the attributes of God—omnipresence, omniscience, and omnipotence. He can be in all places at the same time. That is how he is simultaneously fully present in you and fully present in other believers throughout the world. The Holy Spirit knows all things. Nothing is beyond his grasp. He is fully dialed in on the past, the present, and the future, including all matters pertaining to your life. The Holy Spirit possesses unlimited power—he is all the divine superpowers rolled into one, and then some. And the Holy Spirit, the source of all this divine power, resides in you because you follow Jesus.

So let's dig down and get more specific about what it means to experience the superpowers of the Holy Spirit. Although the Holy Spirit is infinitely creative and works in an unlimited number of ways, Scripture demonstrates at least six key "power points" that are available to us to move mountains in our lives: conviction, intercession, guidance, comfort, gifting, and transformation.

Conviction

This may be the first of the Holy Spirit's powers many of us can recall experiencing. Even before the Holy Spirit takes up residence within us through faith in Jesus, his power is at work on our behalf. Paul told us, "No one can say, 'Jesus is Lord,' except by the Holy Spirit"

(1 Corinthians 12:3). Because our human condition keeps us from seeing our sin and our need for a Savior, the only way we can come to faith is through the convicting work of the Holy Spirit.

We see this aspect of the Holy Spirit's power in the book of Acts when Luke recorded the confession of a woman named Lydia. He wrote, "The Lord opened her heart to respond to Paul's message" (Acts 16:14). If you have received forgiveness of your sins, it is because, at some point in your life, the Holy Spirit hovered over you and opened your heart to see and receive the message.

As a pastor there have been times when I have shared the gospel as plainly and convincingly as I know how, and some people responded while others seemed completely uninterested or unaffected. In this instance the Spirit opened the hearts of some and not of others. That is my only explanation. If the Holy Spirit opened your heart to see your need for the gospel, whisper a little, "Thank you, Holy Spirit." This is a sign of the Spirit's power at work in your life.

Intercession

When we are stuck in a valley, when we feel hopeless, when we want to pray but don't even know what to say, the Holy Spirit steps in and helps us through intercession. The apostle Paul wrote:

> The Spirit helps us in our weakness. We do not know what we ought to pray for, but the Spirit himself

intercedes for us through wordless groans. . . . because the Spirit intercedes for God's people in accordance with the will of God. (Romans 8:26–27)

Have you ever been so discouraged, so hurt, so overwhelmed with sorrow, that when you tried to pray, the only thing that came out was groans? Well, if the Holy Spirit is in you, he will search your heart, identify what you need, and intercede on your behalf. He takes your wordless groans and makes them his own, converting them into a prayer for you that is aligned with the Father's will for you.

There have been numerous occasions in my life when my heart was broken and my spirit was crushed. With my face buried in my hands and tears streaming down my face, the only sounds I could make were groans. The Holy Spirit within me interceded for me in those moments, taking on the burdens I carried that were too heavy for words, and turned my unintelligible sighs into prayers to the Father on my behalf. Little did I know it at the time, but looking back, I can say that these became some of my most effective prayers, releasing God's power in my life in undeniable ways.

Guidance

One of the keys to an empowered life is being able to keep moving forward, always taking the next step to live into God's revealed will. But to move forward in faith, you need guidance, especially when you come to a proverbial fork in the road. At times such as this, you have access to the guidance of the Holy Spirit, who can give you insights and direction on which path to take, further your resolve to take it, and boost your confidence that you will end up in the place God intended for you. When you are in the middle of a gnarly storm, seeking the Holy Spirit's guidance gives you a heightened sense of discernment on how to navigate yourself and others to more peaceful waters.

How will you do all of this? Through the power of the Holy Spirit within you. Jesus told us, "When the Spirit of truth comes, he will guide you into all truth" (John 16:13 ESV). The Holy Spirit is the gentle whisper that speaks directly to our spirits (1 Kings 19:12) when our hearts are open and our souls are still.

The psalmist proclaimed that God's Word "is a lamp for my feet, a light on my path" (Psalm 119:105). The kind of lamp the psalmist used here as a metaphor was fueled by oil and provided only enough light to help the one who carried it take a next step. No floodlight, no high beams, no spotlight—just enough light to keep moving in the right direction. The Holy Spirit is our lamp, residing within us to guide our next step, one at a time.

This is especially important to remember when others may be trying to lead us in the wrong direction. Even then, the Holy Spirit is there to redirect us. Listen to the words of John:

I am writing these things to you about those who are trying to lead you astray. As for you, the anointing you received from him remains in you, and you do not need anyone to teach you. But as his anointing teaches you about all things and as that anointing is real, not counterfeit—just as it has taught you, remain in him. (1 John 2:26–27)

The Holy Spirit remains in us just as he remained in Jesus. If we remain in the Holy Spirit—meaning we are surrendered to and aligned with what he desires for us—he will guide and teach us, illuminating the ancient words of Scripture to give us a strong sense of the next step we need to take.

I wrestled with discerning a next step recently in connection with leading the people I serve in the midst of social upheaval and intense racial tension in our country. It seemed no matter which decision I made, it was going to offend a group of people and stalemate our ability to make progress. To do nothing would be to accept the status quo of injustice. I knew that wasn't right. But I felt stuck and uncertain of how to move forward. I was reading Ephesians 2 looking for guidance when I came across this passage:

For [Jesus] himself is our peace, who has made the two groups one and has destroyed the barrier, the dividing wall of hostility, by setting aside in his flesh the law with its commands and regulations. His purpose was to create in himself one new humanity out of the two, thus making peace, and in one body to reconcile both of them to God through the cross, by which he put to death their hostility. (vv. 14–16)

Jesus is not only against racial injustice; he went to the cross to put an end to it. In this moment, God's Spirit whispered to my spirit, giving me the next step I needed to take: *Randy, rise above the noise of hatred. Don't align yourself with a political party or any voice from the old humanity. Jesus has already given you the road map. Stay off of social media for the time being, and with your African American brothers and sisters in Christ, activate a plan with the gospel at the center of it all.* With confidence I took this direction, and the impact so far has been nothing short of powerful.

The Holy Spirit is with you every moment, and you can rely on him for guidance from one moment to the next. To receive guidance, it is essential to be in a posture of listening, especially as you spend time in God's Word and prayer. When you do, he will keep his promise and guide you into all truth.

Comfort

Of the eighty-seven psalms attributed to David, thirty-three are laments. Each one begins with the words "O God!" David then went on to describe the dilemma he was facing that prompted that particular lament. The one I relate to most is Psalm 69. His words are those of a man overcome with anxiety and depression:

> Save me, O God,
> > for the waters have come up to my neck.
> I sink in the miry depths,
> > where there is no foothold.
> I have come into the deep waters;
> > the floods engulf me.
> I am worn out calling for help;
> > my throat is parched.
> My eyes fail,
> > looking for my God. (vv. 1–3)

I take great comfort in knowing that a man after God's own heart, as David is called in Acts 13:22, prayed with such raw vulnerability and honesty. It gives the rest of us permission to do the same. And when we find ourselves in a dark season of hardship or loss, Jesus reminds us we are not alone in our lament.

Jesus said, "And I will pray the Father, and he shall give you another Comforter, that he may abide with you for ever" (John 14:16 KJV). Jesus was speaking of the Holy Spirit. When you are drowning in depression or overwhelmed by waves of anxiety, don't you just want to wrap yourself up in a large, overstuffed comforter? The Holy Spirit is that comforter, but instead of wrapping himself around you on the outside, he wraps himself around your spirit, where the pain and hurt resides.

How does the Holy Spirit do this? The word *comforter* can also be translated "advocate." An advocate is someone bigger and stronger than us who sticks up for us. When the voices in our head—or of other imperfect humans, or of the spiritual forces of this dark world (Ephesians 6:10)—seek to undermine our identity in Christ and our worth before God, we have a bigger and louder voice that stands up for us. Just knowing that should bring us so much comfort!

The apostle Paul told us:

> The Spirit you received does not make you slaves, so that you live in fear again; rather, the Spirit you received brought about your adoption to sonship. And by him we cry, "Abba, Father." The Spirit himself testifies with our spirit that we are God's children. (Romans 8:15–16)

Regardless of your circumstances, you can take comfort in the fact that your identity, your worth, and your eternal security are not up for grabs. The Holy Spirit, who will never leave you, wraps your spirit in a warm blanket, surrounds your heart with a thick wall of protection and comfort, and says, "Everything is going to be okay." When you tune your heart to listen only to that voice, the Comforter drowns out all the other voices and noise, calming you in the most powerful way. And then fear will subside.

Gifting

The Holy Spirit is a giver of gifts—spiritual gifts. The apostle Paul wrote:

> Now about the gifts of the Spirit, brothers and sisters, I do not want you to be uninformed. . . . There are different kinds of gifts, but the same Spirit distributes them. . . . Now to each one the manifestation of the Spirit is given for the common good. (1 Corinthians 12:1, 4, 7)

When we come to faith in Jesus, the Holy Spirit gives us spiritual gifts to use in collaboration with the spiritual gifts of others in Christ's new family. These gifts empower us to fulfill the will of God in our lives. Here is a list of most of the gifts referred to in the New Testament:

- **Leadership:** the gift to lead and care for people
- **Administration:** the gift to organize, direct, and implement plans
- **Teaching:** the gift to communicate and instruct others
- **Knowledge:** the gift of seeing and retaining truth
- **Wisdom:** the gift of applying truth to everyday life and decisions

- **Prophecy:** the gift of insight into future events
- **Discernment:** the gift to clearly recognize and distinguish between good and evil
- **Exhortation:** the gift to uplift and motivate others as well as challenge and rebuke
- **Shepherding:** the gift to nurture, care for, and guide other people
- **Faith:** the gift to believe and trust in God's will without reservation
- **Evangelism:** the gift of sharing one's faith with others
- **Apostleship:** the gift of raising up leaders and guiding a movement
- **Service:** the gift of providing help and aid where needed to achieve the mission
- **Mercy:** the gift to love and assist those who are suffering
- **Giving:** the gift of generosity
- **Hospitality:** the gift of welcoming strangers and entertaining guests

The spiritual gift or gifts you receive from the Holy Spirit might be something entirely new, or it could be a repurposing of a gift you already have and are using in some way. When you receive a new gift, you find you now have the ability and desire to do something you might not have been able to do or wanted to do before you came to Christ. Or, the Holy Spirit supercharges an ability you were born with and redirects it toward God's purposes. With the Holy Spirit's power living and active within you, you are now equipped to contribute in new ways to God's kingdom work and to navigate God's will for your life.

Perhaps you already know your spiritual gifts or have a sense of them, but if not, one of the best ways to discover what your gifts might be is to ask other believers who know you. You might start the conversation by showing them the list of gifts above and asking them which one or ones they think you might possess based on what they've observed and noticed about you. When you ask, don't guide them in any way. Once they make their choice, ask them to share an example of how they have witnessed you using this spiritual gift. After talking to eight to ten people, chances are good that certain themes will emerge to point you toward one or more specific spiritual gifts. If others in your life have seen your spiritual gifts in action, then they have no doubt been positively impacted by them when you are at your best.

There is soul-level power in knowing your unique spiritual gifts, because at the core of your giftedness from God is a sense of purpose. And a sense of purpose is a key ingredient to a happy, healthy, empowered life. Thank you, Holy Spirit!

Transformation

Transformation is perhaps the Holy Spirit's biggest superpower. It is one thing to have external circumstances in our lives removed or changed so they don't get in our way; it is another thing entirely when we change from the inside out and are equipped to overcome the obstacles we face.

Without question, my favorite ministry of the Holy Spirit is his transforming work in our lives. The Bible refers to the evidence of this transformation as the "fruit of the Spirit" (Galatians 5:22). It is the outcome of the Spirit's working in us as we abide in Christ (John 15).

So what is the fruit of the Spirit? It is what love looks like when lived out in us. Paul gave us a list of these virtues of transformation in his letter to the believers living in the ancient city of Galatia:

> But the fruit of the Spirit is love, joy, peace, forbearance, kindness, goodness, faithfulness, gentleness and self-control. Against such things there is no law. (Galatians 5:22–23)

Odd as it may sound, the best image or metaphor for the fruits of the Spirit probably isn't a bowl of fruit. Rather, imagine a glass of wine in the hands of a sommelier or wine steward. The sommelier picks up the wine glass by the stem and gives it a swirl. She places her nose fully within the glass and breathes in deeply. She gives it one more swirl and takes a sip. Then she might say, "This is a cabernet sauvignon from the Napa region. I am picking up hints of licorice, vanilla, and blackberry."

On this occasion, Paul, the spiritual sommelier, went through a similar routine and said of the church, "This is a glass of love from the vineyards of Jesus. I am picking up hints of joy, peace, and patience." Instead of apples and oranges, something more like wine is the image Paul had in mind when he wrote about the fruits of the Spirit. Winemaking is complex, and grapes on the vine go through a tremendous transformation process over time to become a great glass of wine. Similarly, Paul wrote about the fruits of the Spirit to convey the expectation that as we grow in love of Christ and others, our lives become fragrant with the aroma of transformation—the sweet-smelling virtues of love, joy, peace, forbearance, kindness, goodness, faithfulness, gentleness, and self-control.

How does the divine vigneron pull this off? There is so much to say here, but let me touch on just one aspect I find especially encouraging. It has to do with what science reveals about the power of relational attachment and character formation.

In the center of the human brain, God placed a mass of gray matter we call the thalamus. Among other things, this is the part of the brain that processes relational attachments to others. When our attachments are overflowing with healthy love, the thalamus receives a sensation that it then passes on to the cerebral cortex, the part of the brain in which identity and character are formed. When the love we receive from others is strong and consistent, it produces the character traits Paul identified as the fruit of the Spirit. In other words, loving relationships have the power to literally re-form and reshape the brain in ways that change who we are—our identity and character.

With this in mind, lean in and listen to Paul's prayer for the believers in the city of Ephesus:

> For this reason I kneel before the Father, from whom every family in heaven and on earth derives its name. I pray that out of his glorious riches he may strengthen you with power through his Spirit in your inner being, so that Christ may dwell in your hearts through faith. And I pray that you, being rooted and established in love, may have power, together with all the Lord's holy people, to grasp how wide and long and high and deep is the love of Christ, and to know this love that surpasses knowledge—that you may be filled to the measure of all the fullness of God. (Ephesians 3:14–19)

The heart of Paul's prayer is that the inner work of the Holy Spirit will allow us to grasp how much God loves us. When this happens, we are already on our way to becoming all God intended us to become—filled with the fullness of God.

Neurotheologian Jim Wilder told us, "With a loving attachment that will not let us go, we can develop a fully formed, joyful, and Christlike character."[3] When we allow ourselves to experience God's love through the proximity and power of the Holy Spirit, our thalamus receives a positive sensation and forwards it to our cerebral cortex for interpretation—which, ultimately, leads to positive transformation.

This truth about attachment, which science has only recently been able to document, was conveyed thousands of years ago by Jesus, who used the analogy of a vine and branches:

> I am the true vine. . . . Remain in me, as I also remain in you. . . . As the Father has loved me, so have I loved you. Now remain in my love. If you keep my commands, you will remain in my love, just as I have kept my Father's commands and remain in his love. I have told you this so that my joy may be in you and that your joy may be complete. (John 15:1, 4, 9–11)

As we remain connected to the vine of Christ, we receive the nutrients of his love directly into our lives. This loving attachment stimulates growth in our lives that strengthens our identity and ultimately produces joy.

After Paul finished listing the nine fruits (virtuous qualities) available to followers of Jesus through the ministry of the Holy Spirit, he concluded with this statement: "Against such things there is no law" (Galatians 5:23). What does this mean? It means that you and I can't develop these beautiful virtues by having a judge rule them as requirements. "You must be joyful or go to jail." It doesn't work that way. In other words, we can't produce these virtues from the outside in. Such radical transformation can only come about from the inside out. Paul called this metamorphosis the "renewing of your mind" (Romans 12:2). When the Spirit is released to do his work within us, we become transformed people who look a little more like Jesus every day.

It is the Holy Spirit who empowers us to:

- unconditionally cherish and forgive others (*love*);
- have inner contentment and purpose in spite of our circumstances (*joy*);
- be free from anxiety because things are right with our relationships (*peace*);
- forbear under the unavoidable pressures of life (*patience*);
- act positively toward others (*kindness*);
- be full of integrity (*goodness*);
- be loyal and trustworthy to the people God has placed in our lives (*faithfulness*);
- be thoughtful, considerate, and calm in our relationships with others (*gentleness*); and
- restrain ourselves from destructive behaviors (*self-control*).

When we yield our lives to the will of the Father, just as Jesus modeled for us, we will be transformed, and our lives will become increasingly fruitful.

Conviction, intercession, guidance, comfort, gifting,

transformation—these are the superpowers of the Holy Spirit. Have you felt convicted about anything recently? If so, you've experienced power. Have you received the guidance you needed to make a decision? If so, you've experienced power. Have you experienced God's comfort or witnessed even the smallest sign of transformation in your life? If so, you've experienced power. The superpowers of the Holy Spirit are always at work, always available to you, ready to help you take that next step from powerlessness to real empowerment. The Holy Spirit is the power source that raised Jesus from the dead, and the Holy Spirit's power is available to you, right now. With just a little faith in God, you can move mountains.

MOVING MOUNTAINS

A man stepped out of a crowd, knelt before Jesus, and begged him to heal his son. The man's son was experiencing severe seizures brought on by demon possession. I can totally relate to the anguish of this dad, can't you? The father had initially brought his son to the disciples, but they had been unable to heal the boy. Jesus had the boy brought to him and rebuked the demon. At once, the boy was completely restored to wholeness and health.

Earlier Jesus had given the disciples authority to drive out impure spirits and even raise people from the dead (Matthew 10:1, 8). So they were naturally confused when they weren't able to heal the boy. What went wrong? Listen to Jesus' answer:

> He replied, "Because you have so little faith. Truly I tell you, if you have faith as small as a mustard seed, you can say to this mountain, 'Move from here to there,' and it will move. Nothing will be impossible for you." (17:20–21)

What was Jesus really saying here? It is the same admonition he had for the disciples when they were freaked-out during the storm on the Sea of Galilee. After Jesus calmed the storm, he turned to the disciples and said, "Do you still have no faith?" (Mark 4:40). However, in this instance, the issue was not so much about the quantity of their faith as it was the quality of their faith. Jesus said it would take only a small amount of faith to move a mountain. The quantity of faith was not the issue, because it was not faith that would ultimately move the mountain. The power they needed wasn't coming from them but from the Holy Spirit.

We pray to the Father to discern his will, and then we rely on the Holy Spirit to achieve it in and through us. Our faith is not in ourselves but in God. Prayer is the primary tool we use to tap into the power of God within us. There are no limits for those of us who believe, because faith is not about what we can do, but what God can do through us. Dynamite!

Now, a brief word about moving mountains. To me, that's right up there with the notion that we have access to the same power that raised people from the dead. Is that really possible? For some insights, let's take a brief peek back into the Old Testament.

In 538 BC a guy named Zerubbabel led a group of Jewish people from exile in Babylon to rebuild the temple in Jerusalem. In the process they had to overcome many obstacles and threats from the surrounding nations. Zechariah, the prophet, spoke for God these words:

> "What are you, mighty mountain? Before Zerubbabel you will become level ground. Then he will bring out the capstone to shouts of 'God bless it! God bless it!'"
> Then the word of the LORD came to me: "The hands of Zerubbabel have laid the foundation of this temple; his hands will also complete it. Then you will know that the LORD Almighty has sent me to you." (Zechariah 4:7–9)

Here, the mountain referred to an obstacle—to the opposition God's people were facing from outsiders who didn't want Israel to gain the upper hand. I don't know many people today who need to move a literal mountain, but I do know a ton of people who need to move an obstacle of some kind from their lives. How does the proverbial mountain that is holding us back from God's best for us get removed? Zechariah told us:

This is the word of the LORD to Zerubbabel: "Not by
might nor by power, but by my Spirit," says the LORD
Almighty. (v. 6)

The mountains we face are not moved by our own
might or power, but by God's Spirit within us. We don't
accomplish feats of great power in the Christian life by
trying harder but by *yielding* harder to the will of God. It
is only under these conditions that the Spirit, who could
easily move a physical mountain, goes to work to tear
down the metaphorical mountains or obstacles in our lives.

Sadly it sometimes takes a lifetime for most of us
to really understand this truth. The yoke of Jesus is not
burdensome but easy (Matthew 11:30). To experience
it, we have to abandon ourselves completely to his plan.
Without conditions, we unclench our fists and open them
up to receive God's will. Then we step back and wait to
see how God accomplishes on earth what we thought
could only be achieved in heaven . . . right in our lives.

How will we rise from powerlessness? How will we
ascend above the circumstances that hold us down? How
will we overcome the mountain of obstacles in front of
us? How will we either level the miles of rock that stand
in our way or scale to the top of them and achieve the
very purpose for which we were placed on this earth?
Dynamite! We will do so through the same power that
raised Jesus from the dead—the Holy Spirit who rests on
his followers.

MY MOUNTAINS

Through access to the Holy Spirit's power, I have risen from a place of powerlessness to a place of increased health, vitality, and purpose. The ominous mountain of betrayal and depression that intimidated me for two years has been transformed into a beautiful channel through which God's plans and power can flow freely.

After a lot of prayer, counsel, and personal work, I finally came to the place where I could truly say, as Joseph did, that what my betrayers intended for harm, God intended for good (Genesis 50:20). It was the betrayal of Joseph's brothers that led him to Egypt, which led him to become second in command over all of Egypt, which ultimately led to the saving of many lives from a famine. I can now see something like this being worked out in my life.

Although I do not believe God caused the betrayal that devastated me, I do believe he is using it to achieve his will in my life. As a person who thrives in warm climates and struggles with colder ones, it's unlikely I would have considered moving from San Antonio to Kansas City before the betrayal. And yet I have no doubt that this is where God wanted me to be to achieve his will and call on my life. Let me share just one example of how I have risen by experiencing the power of God in and through me.

In leaning in and discerning God's will for my new assignment, I got a strong sense that the people in Kansas City struggled with margin—both with their time and with their finances. I had a vision that our church could play a role in uniting area pastors and churches to help people experience real and positive change.

We began by partnering with Ramsey Solutions to slay what we labeled the "Margin Monster." Our plan was to offer their Financial Peace University course in a ten-week series that would teach biblical principles for finding margins with time and money. We set a goal to have 80 percent of our congregation participate in the course. Because my role at the church also involves uniting churches in our city, we set a goal to recruit 100 other churches to join us in this journey. I knew the wind of the Spirit was in this initiative when we not only met but exceeded that goal, recruiting 110 churches.

Here are the results after ten weeks:

- 9,200 credit cards cut up
- $4.7 million saved
- $17.7 million of debt eliminated
- 89 percent of families reported having more conversations about their finances

The last statistic is especially significant when you realize that arguments and stress over finances are often cited as a leading cause of divorce. We were not tackling the margin problem alone, but also uniting and strengthening families by addressing one of their top foes.

By the time we finished this initiative at the end of

2019, I had been in Kansas City for a little over a year. At the start of 2020, the coronavirus hit and decimated economies around the world. Kansas City was hit just as hard, and yet there were literally thousands of people who, as a result of working on their finances, now had an emergency fund set aside to help them weather this storm. The e-mails poured in as people expressed their gratitude for the course, including the timing of it. Some even asked if I knew the virus was coming. I told them if I had known, I would have bought more toilet paper. (You may recall there was a shortage.)

I felt a bit like Joseph, though on a much smaller scale, who had helped the people of Egypt set aside an emergency supply of food to get them through famine. Although we had no idea what was coming, we did our best to align our lives and work with our best understanding of God's will. The Holy Spirit went to work, and . . . dynamite!

On a more personal note, I also learned from Joseph's willingness to forgive the brothers who betrayed him, even though I am not sure the brothers ever forgave themselves. I always wondered when Joseph was able to do this. Twenty-two years had passed from the time his brothers betrayed him to the time they bowed down before him. When in this long and difficult journey was Joseph able to forgive his brothers and put the whole thing behind him?

After reading through the story, I think I found the moment. After Pharaoh appointed Joseph to his leadership position, Joseph married. Before the years of famine hit, he had two boys. I believe it was in this period that Joseph experienced the shift in his heart that took forgiveness from an act of obedience to the genuine release of a burden that weighed him down. The clue comes in the meaning of the names he gave his sons.

He named his firstborn Manasseh. In Hebrew, Manasseh means "forget." Joseph said he gave his son this name because "God has made me forget all my trouble and all my father's household" (Genesis 41:51). That doesn't mean Joseph drew a blank about his past or that he could no longer recall the events that brought him to Egypt or the many things he suffered as a result. When he said he had forgotten all his trouble, I take it to mean he no longer woke up every day thinking about the betrayal. Instead, he was free to focus more on living in the present and cultivating hope for his future. Joseph had not only forgiven; he had forgotten. Forgiveness is an act of obedience; forgetting is the sign that the forgiveness has taken root deep in the soul.

Joseph named his second son Ephraim, which means "twice fruitful." Joseph said he gave his son this name "because God has made me fruitful in the land of my suffering" (v. 52). God had restored what Joseph had lost—times two.

I resonate with both aspects of Joseph's experience— his journey from forgiving to forgetting and becoming more fruitful—because it is precisely what happened to me. Almost two years in, I was able to get to the point where the pain of the past no longer dominated my daily life. I was finally able to not only forgive from the heart, but to forget from the heart. That's when I turned a corner—when I could fully engage in the present and once again be hopeful for the future. As a result, God also made me "twice fruitful." The impact of slaying the "Margin Monster" was only the beginning. I experienced my Manasseh and Ephraim moments, and my mountain moved.

YOUR MOUNTAINS

Wherever you find yourself on the empowerment scale, I hope you now have a greater sense of hope that the same power that raised Christ from the dead—and raised me from a pit to a pinnacle of new purpose—is the same power that resides in you. This is the invitation of God to you.

In Christ, living an empowered life is not only possible but actually expected. Paul put the truth to us this way:

> For we are God's masterpiece. He has created us anew in Christ Jesus, so we can do the good things he planned for us long ago. (Ephesians 2:10 NLT)

Before you were even born, it was your destiny to join God in the amazing work he has planned. If you will join the Father in this work, the Holy Spirit will provide the dynamite required to make it happen.

As you consider what your next steps might be, I have two questions for you to ponder, slowly and prayerfully. As you ponder each one, think of where you are now and envision where you would like to be next.

Do you believe God has a plan and a purpose for your life? For many things in life we have a tendency to act in our own strength. This is the only strength we have to draw on when the focus of our life is on building our own kingdom. But the power of the Holy Spirit is only released in us as we align ourselves with God's will. The Spirit doesn't leave us when we draw on our own power, but the Spirit's power is more or less quenched, untapped, unlit, and sometimes even grieved (Ephesians 5:18; 1 Thessalonians 5:19).

I am fully convinced God has a plan to use you for his kingdom, and I encourage you to allow this truth to preoccupy your mind. Read God's Word with this at the forefront. Talk with others about it. Talk to God about it. Start a journal, recording the impressions you receive in your spirit and the circumstances that might be sending you a clear message about it.

God's plan for you might be anything from a big project or a big change to focusing on personal growth and healing. In fact, many times God's plans for us are not so much an outward assignment as an inward one. God may want to heal deep wounds within you. It might be a wound from a relationship with a parent or sibling, a divorce, sexual abuse, addictions, a personal failure, or any number of things. Although you appear to be functioning fine on the outside, you are not doing well on the inside.

It is God's will for you to be healed of these hurts. Because it is God's will, the Holy Spirit within you can overpower the self-defeating voices in your head and bring complete renewal. Once there is healing on the inside, the floodgates of new power will be released in you, channeled from the inside out to impact other people in positive ways. Therefore, stop trying so hard to move your personal mountain, whatever it is, in your own strength, and yield harder to the will of God and the desires of the Spirit within you.

Is there something God is whispering to your spirit— something he might want you to do, to change, or to stop doing? This is the question I have been waiting to ask since I penned the first words of this book. God has deposited an insane amount of firepower within you. Spiritual dynamite! What does God want to use it for in and through you in this next season of your life?

It might be the miracle of contentment with the season you are in. Where you are may not be where you want to be, but it is where you need to be.

It might be a small win. A series of small wins can equal a huge win.

Or it might be something bigger than you ever

imagined, just as it was when I felt God speaking the word *cities* to me. To be completely transparent, I am now hearing the whisper of the word *world*. Frankly, it doesn't scare me or make me feel any more important. It is not about me. If it were about me, I'd be having visions of God leading me to start a golf outreach or a nap ministry. But if the vision to impact the world is God's will for me, his Spirit will empower whatever he wants me to do. The makings of *His Mighty Strength 2.0*?

God wants to move the mountain in your life. Name it, put it in writing, and then start marching toward it with God's confidence. He has placed the spiritual dynamite within you to turn that mountain into a deep and beautiful canal that channels God's love and God's will through you. I double-dog dare you to light the fuse.

Dancing on Mountains

I crawl into bed around 10:00 p.m. The first thing I notice is the sheets. They had been changed earlier in the day. I let out a sigh of satisfaction. *Ahhh*, nothing quite like fresh sheets. I lay my head on the pillow, actually three pillows because I'm that guy. I bury my head in a nest of down and sigh again. *Ahhh* . . . A few minutes later, Rozanne, my champion and companion for more than forty years, slips into bed next to me. Sigh number three. *Ahhh*.

I am ready to take in my nightly episode on HGTV. On this night, it's my favorite, *House Hunters International*. A couple, slightly older than us, is looking to buy a place in Italy. They walk up a narrow cobblestone street free of automobiles to look at the first of three homes they will visit that day—a traditional Mediterranean villa constructed out of drystone masonry. The antique wooden front door features an iron doorknob, and there are window boxes spilling over with beautiful flowers and vines draping down on the rustic stone. The couple walks to the back of the house that opens to a view of the rolling hills of Tuscany. Breathtaking. Sigh number four, *ahhh*.

As the show comes to an end, the couple is sitting at an outdoor café, sipping espressos and discussing their options. Of the three homes, they select the one just right for them—the same one Rozanne and I would have chosen. Sigh number five. *Ahhh.*

It is the same routine every night. I take a sip of water, remove my glasses, turn off the television, and place the remote control on the nightstand. Then I take the top pillow and place it to my side and lay my head down on the remaining two pillows. And yes, it's sigh number six. *Ahhh,* the end of another good day.

It's been three years now since my season of waking up in the night beating my pillow with my fist out of deep anguish for the awful place I was in. I still have the same pillow—the same exact one—but I'm no longer in an awful place. I have forgiven my betrayers and rarely think about the betrayal. Back then, I couldn't get off the couch; now I dream about getting a place in Italy. I was in a pit, and now I live every day knowing I have a purpose. I was powerless, and now I am empowered to live my calling before my God. I was stuck in a valley, and now I am dancing on a mountaintop.

My nightmares have turned into hopeful dreams. I whisper a heartfelt thank-you to God and breathe out my last sigh for the night before falling fast asleep. *Ahhh.*

WHERE WE'VE BEEN

This book began with an invitation to a journey. I promised I would not come to you as a preacher, but as a fellow traveler, two friends having honest conversations in the back corner of a coffee shop. I hope you feel I have kept that promise.

I also promised to be intensely biblical. Writing about something as weighty and important as accessing the same power that raised Jesus from the dead requires a source of truth greater than a finite human point of view. We need to be anchored in the eternal truth of God's Word.

I was eager to let you in on a fresh discovery I found embedded in the ancient pages of Scripture that reveal what Jesus did for us when he came to this earth. Although I've spent forty-seven years following Jesus, I've only been privy to this knowledge about Jesus for the last six years. Now I want to tell everyone about it.

When Jesus voluntarily left the heavens to come walk among us, he did three things to show us the way to live an empowered life. Jesus *emptied* himself of his divine attributes to take on the constraints of humanity. He did this out of his great love for us. He became vulnerable to show us the way to God and the path to amazing power. We are now invited to acknowledge our vulnerability and to place the control of our lives in the hands of God.

Jesus *aligned* himself with the Father's will. He didn't make a move or even speak a word unless the Father instructed him to do so. It was his passion to fulfill the will of God for his life, which ultimately led him to the cross. Jesus now invites us to follow this same pattern by surrendering our will to the will of the Father.

Jesus was *empowered* by the Holy Spirit. At Jesus'

baptism, the Holy Spirit came down and remained with Jesus to give him access to divine power. That is how he fulfilled the will of God, performed miracles, healed the sick, and was resurrected from the dead.

Throughout his life, Jesus taught us the secret of accessing his mighty strength. When we align our lives with the will of the Father, the Holy Spirit empowers us to fulfill it. Through the Spirit's power within us, we will move mountains, be conduits for miracles, and even rise from the dead when Jesus returns to earth.

It was the discovery of this pattern in the life of Jesus that first led me to write this book. I wanted you to see what Jesus did for us and how much he gave up in order to offer us the life we were intended to live in God. And so I got to work and drafted a manuscript, focusing especially on the theological ideas I found most interesting.

Then the bottom dropped out of my life, and I fell from an 8 to a 2 on the empowerment scale. The manuscript I'd started no longer held much interest for me. I didn't even have the capacity to open my laptop most days, much less pursue abstract ideas about God's power. Eventually, at the advice of my wife and publisher, I threw my dry theological treatise in the trash and started over. Now, instead of the words coming out of my head, they were flowing from my life—from my soul to yours.

I made what was for me a very difficult decision and promised to be transparent and vulnerable. The word *transparent* means to be "clear enough to be seen through."[1] I wanted to share the real me with all my doubts, struggles, and failures. I have stood emotionally naked before you, and, to be honest, at times it has felt embarrassing.

Vulnerability can be uncomfortable. The dictionary says a vulnerable person is one who is "capable of being wounded."[2] Who wants that? My preference would be for you to see me only as a strong and virtually invincible pastor and leader. Even though I wanted to be truly vulnerable, there were some lingering fears that it might come back to bite me or backfire in some way and hurt me even deeper. This is vulnerability.

I decided to take the risk in the hope that it might help you. When I think of the Son of God hanging naked on a cross, transparent and vulnerable before a crowd of mostly gawkers, I am confident that risking vulnerability is God's will for me. If I am right, then the Holy Spirit will empower me to see it through, come what may. So far . . . so good.

WHERE ARE YOU NOW?

At the beginning of our journey together, I invited you to plot yourself on the empowerment scale. Where did you place yourself? Perhaps you were at a 1 or 2, stuck in the valley of despair and struggle. I really do know how you feel. If you are like me, you may have concluded that there was no way up. This was it; this was your lot in life.

How do you feel now? I pray that Jesus has cleared a path for you to rise above your circumstances, to exit the valley and start heading up to the mountains. I pray you have taken him up on his promise and are willing at least to begin taking a few steps on this path.

Maybe you placed yourself right in the middle of the empowerment scale. You were getting through the days but had long given up that there might be more. You weren't stuck in the valley, but the elevation of your base camp wasn't that impressive. Where are you right now? I pray you are dreaming again. I pray you sense your best days are still ahead of you.

Maybe you initially ranked yourself pretty high on the empowerment scale. If so, my prayer for you is two-fold. One, that you are confident your footing comes from your identity in Christ, your purpose comes from the will of God, and your strength comes from the Holy Spirit within you. I got pretty high up the mountain in my own strength, but I also fell hard and fast when a crisis hit I couldn't handle. Two, if you are firmly anchored in your relationship with God, I hope you are starting to envision climbing even higher. In Christ, the sky is truly the limit. I am pretty confident God has more in store for you.

When I first agreed to write this book, I plotted myself as an 8 on the empowerment scale. Then a betrayal knocked on my door. I opened the door and grabbed betrayal by the hand and let it take me down to a 2. I wallowed there for eight solid months. Over a period of two years, God has led me right back to a solid 8 on the empowerment scale. I'm breathing in the fresh air of mountain living once again.

But things are different than they were before. Today, I live with the acute awareness of my weakness. I live with the reminder that if I take my gaze from God and trust in my own strength, I am susceptible to another free fall. I don't want to go back down to that place again.

The apostle Paul was aware of his weakness and on three occasions asked God to take it from him. He recorded God's gentle whisper back to him:

My grace is sufficient for you, for my power is made perfect in weakness. (2 Corinthians 12:9)

Paul eventually stopped praying for his weakness to be removed and instead made this declaration:

Therefore, I will boast all the more gladly about my weaknesses, so that Christ's power may rest on me. . . . For when I am weak, then I am strong. (vv. 9–10)

My current state of empowerment doesn't come from

self-sufficiency. With Paul, I can testify, "I can do all this through [Christ] who gives me strength" (Philippians 4:13). This truth keeps me tethered to God daily. I hope you feel the same way.

LET'S KEEP GOING

Wherever you find yourself on the empowerment scale, I trust that you are reaching out for the power that is available to you, and that you want what God is offering. I pray you are allowing hope a chance to take root in your heart, to believe that things can and will be different for you. This is the turn that will point you in a new direction. You will be facing true north, and it will lead you upward. Just keep putting one foot in front of the other.

Let's commit together to keep going and keep moving forward in faith. The principles Jesus taught and lived will progressively move us upward to a more empowered life. I join with the apostle Paul in praying this prayer for you as you continue your journey:

> I pray that the eyes of your heart may be enlightened
> in order that you may know the hope to which he has
> called you, the riches of his glorious inheritance in his
> holy people, and his incomparably great power for us
> who believe. That power is the same as the mighty

strength he exerted when he raised Christ from the dead and seated him at his right hand in the heavenly realms. (Ephesians 1:18–20)

God's mighty strength is available to you. Don't settle for being stuck in the valley. You are destined to dance on mountains.

Acknowledgments

This has been the most challenging book I have written to date. It started out as a fresh theological discovery regarding the life of Jesus. It was so exhilarating to finally connect the dots on the collision of Jesus' full divinity with his full humanity that made sense and provided such a clear road map for us.

From there it became a 2,200-word manuscript that I preached on an Easter Sunday that resulted in 286 people spontaneously getting baptized. From there it became a book contract to write a 40,000-word treatise on the idea. Everything was "up and to the right."

Then I encountered the personal crisis that left me feeling powerless. Writing a book on tapping into the same power that raised Jesus from the dead seemed comical at best. I certainly tried, but the ink in my pen was dry.

I finally forced myself to put out a full manuscript

that would fill the intellectual intrigue of my seminary geek friends. That manuscript was all but thrown in the trash, and we started over. There was a wall built up in me that wouldn't allow the content of the book to first run through my own soul. Very unusual for my temperament.

What you hold in your hand is the product of a complete rewrite. The raw vulnerability on some of the pages was a bit tough for me, but in the end, I am glad I shared what was really going on in my life. This is the book God intended for me to write; he just didn't let me in on it until later in the journey. I'm totally cool with that.

I didn't get to this place alone. There is a community around me that held up my arms in the heat of the battle so I could win. I want to acknowledge some of them now.

Ron Doornink, Tom Irwin, and Mike Reilly graciously became my personal board of directors. These guys led me through one of the most difficult seasons of my life. They supported me while shooting it to me straight. They saw me at my worst and yet never gave up on me. Thank you.

There is a very special group of pastors from around the country who were flat out there for me. I am a passionate member of their tribe. They reminded me that I was not alone. I won't list their names, but when they read this, they will know I am talking about them.

My neighbors in Cordillera Ranch will always have a special place in my heart. It is a very special plot of land on our planet where rich, loyal community abounds. There are a few names that I must call out for the sheer volume of time they invested in both Rozanne and me. For most of them, I was their pastor. But in this season, the tables were turned, and they pastored us—Todd and Catherine Gerch, James and Maria Sayers, Bob and Donna Biddle, Ron and Martha Doornink, Tom and Janie Irwin, Walter and Cheryl Ratliff, Van and Jodi Wilkerson, Mark and Pam McCurly, Ray and Margaret Putney, David and Gail Sanders, Steve and Nancye Drukker, and David Cottrell. Thank you.

Speaking of neighbors, I must let you know how crazy I am about my Cottonwood Canyon neighbors here in Kansas City. We are a part of a fresh, loving, missional community of believers led by John and Barbara Markert. If we could multiply this small spiritual micro community a million times over in our world, Jesus wins. A special shout-out to my neighbor and lead stagehand, Chris Markert, for your friendship and sincere love for God and people. What a joy to have Scott and Donita Jones back in our lives. Roots are like a balm that heals deep wounds.

I must acknowledge Westside Family Church, where I now serve as their lead teaching pastor. They are a very, very special group of people—full of faith, passionate about all things Jesus, unselfishly committed to serve the "Big C" church, and deeply committed to serve the last, the lost, and the least. Small-minded thinking does not rule the roost in this radical group of Christ's followers. A shout-out of gratitude to the pastors, staff, and congregation I serve alongside.

I would never survive the rigors of being a pastor of a large congregation along with all the other initiatives God invites me into if I didn't have a very dedicated and loyal assistant. Laura Saville has been that for both me and Rozanne. She manages my schedule, deals with thousands of folks on my behalf, tries to stay at least a couple of steps ahead of me, and embraces my unique idiosyncrasies with a smile on her face. Thank you.

For twenty years now I have had the privilege of writing for HarperCollins Christian Publishing. They are an incredible partner. I want to thank CEO Mark Schoenwald for his belief in me. Back in the '90s, I got to be Mark's pastor when God sent him and his family on a radical faith journey that has led him to this massive role of influence. God has been writing a bigger story all along that we are just now getting glimpses into.

Right now I am shaking my head in disbelief at the Christlike patience Jessica Wong showed to me each time the deadline for this book got pushed out even further. Crowns in heaven await you—of this I am sure.

Truth-telling time: you would not be holding this book in your hand if it were not for my editor Christine Anderson. She is crazy gifted in the craft of writing, but also drinks from a deep well of spiritual insight. She was more than a coach for me. She painstakingly pastored me through each page. No one has ever pushed me as hard as Christine to bring out my very best. Thank you, I think. I am also grateful for the new journey with my agent, Don

Gates. Thanks for your support on this book and for the many more to come. Let's do this.

I have been blessed beyond measure with the most incredible family. We have four children who are now all grown up. I am not only proud of each of them but blown away at how proud and supportive they are of their imperfect father. Jennifer, David, Stephen, Austin—you cannot know how much joy and meaning you bring to my life (which now includes Desmond and Gretchen). To my two grand-children, Ava and Crew, and the many more to come, you provide so much motivation for Baba to keep going!

Let me just say it—I love my wife! Over forty years ago my parents said to me, "Better marry this one 'cause this kind doesn't come around often." They were so, so right! Rozanne (also known as Corkie by her family and closest friends) has loved me with a fierce and loyal love that goes beyond my comprehension given my frailties and short-comings. No one has believed in me more than Rozanne. You can reach crazy heights with this kind of support. In the truest sense of the word, we are one. To the end.

Finally, I want to acknowledge my God—Father, Son, and Holy Spirit. I became a Christian on June 14, 1974, at the invitation of Ray and Mary Graham. I had no idea how life changing this decision would be, with so much more to come. I have truly experienced the same power that raised Jesus from the dead.

RANDY FRAZEE

NOTES

Chapter 1: What Jesus Left Behind

1. Roger E. Olson, *The Mosaic of Christian Belief: Twenty Centuries of Unity and Diversity*, 2nd ed. (Downers Grove, IL: InterVarsity Press, 2016), 236.
2. See the New American Standard Bible (NASB) and the English Standard Version (ESV).
3. Step 1, "12 Steps," https://www.12step.com/12steps.

Chapter 4: How We Need to Live

1. Karen Abbott, "The Daredevil of Niagara Falls," *Smithsonian Magazine*, October 18, 2011, https://www.smithsonianmag.com/history/the-daredevil-of-niagara-falls-110492884/.
2. Dan Stevers, "Charles Blondin: Faith on a Wire," May 17, 2010, YouTube video, https://www.youtube.com/watch?v=dTuyKQVIM3E.
3. I also had the privilege of adapting his book

Renovation of the Heart for students. See Dallas
Willard and Randy Frazee, *Renovation of the Heart:
An Interactive Student Edition* (Colorado Springs:
NavPress, 2005).

4. Dallas Willard, *Hearing God* (Downers Grove, IL:
   InterVarsity Press, 2012), 222.
5. Frederick B. Meyer, *The Secret of Guidance* (Chicago:
   Moody, 1997, 2010), 42.
6. Willard, *Hearing God*, 115.
7. Willard, 118, 130.
8. E. Stanley Jones, *A Song of Ascents: A Spiritual
   Autobiography* (Nashville: Abingdon, 1979), 190.
9. Willard, *Hearing God*, 92, 221.
10. Meyer, *The Secret of Guidance*, 18.
11. Meyer, 28–29.
12. Willard, *Hearing God*, 224.
13. Abbott, "The Daredevil of Niagara Falls."

Chapter 5: How Jesus Rose from the Dead

1. Georg Braumann, "Advocate, Paraclete, Helper," *New
   International Dictionary of New Testament Theology*,
   ed. Colin Brown (Grand Rapids, MI: Zondervan, 1975,
   1986), 1:88–89.
2. Some people think that perhaps the miracle at the
   wedding in Cana took place before Jesus' baptism
   because Mark's gospel says that after Jesus' baptism he
   was led into the wilderness and stayed there for forty
   days. I found this article to be helpful in clearing the
   matter: Ron Dudek, "Wilderness or Wedding?" Answers
   in Genesis, June 19, 2012, https://answersingenesis.org
   /jesus/wilderness-or-wedding/.
3. "The Miracles of Jesus," John 2:1–12, *NIV Zondervan*

Study Bible, ed. D. A. Carson (Grand Rapids, MI: Zondervan, 2015), 1765.

4. Oxford Languages, s.v. "rah-rah," lexico.com, https://www.lexico.com/en/definition/rah-rah.

5. "Neuroplasticity," infogram.com, https://infogram.com/everyday-examples-of-neuroplasticity-1hxj488nnvmd4vg.

6. Corrie ten Boom, quoted on Goodreads, https://www.goodreads.com/quotes/110765.

7. "Hidden Meaning of 11 World's Most Famous Logos," *Economic Times*, July 24, 2017, https://economictimes.indiatimes.com/industry/services/advertising/hidden-meaning-of-11-worlds-most-famous-logos/nike/slideshow/59738997.cms.

8. *Ultraman Ginga*, season 1, episode 11, "Kimi no Mirai," directed by Yûichi Abe, written by Keiichi Hasegawa, aired December 18, 2013, on TV Tokyo.

Chapter 6: How We Will Rise

1. Amy Lively, "What Is the Purpose of the Panama Canal?" *USA Today*, March 13, 2018, https://traveltips.usatoday.com/purpose-panama-canal-63793.html.

2. *Merriam-Webster Dictionary* (1997), s.v. "dynamite."

3. Jim Wilder, *Renovated: God, Dallas Willard, and the Church That Transforms* (Colorado Springs: NavPress, 2020), 90.

Afterword: Dancing on Mountains

1. *Merriam-Webster Dictionary*, s.v. "transparent."

2. *Merriam-Webster Dictionary*, s.v. "vulnerable."

ABOUT THE AUTHOR

Randy Frazee is the lead pastor at Westside Family Church in Kansas City. A front-runner and innovator in spiritual formation and biblical community, Randy is the architect of The Story and Believe church engagement campaigns. He is also the author of *The Heart of the Story*; *Think, Act, Be Like Jesus*; *What Happens After You Die*; *The Connecting Church 2.0*; and *The Christian Life Profile Assessment*. He and his wife, Rozanne, live in Kansas City, Kansas.